WIKIS, [   ], AND NETWORKS

Creating Connections
for Conflict-Prone Settings

Author
Rebecca Linder

Project Directors
Frederick Barton
Karin von Hippel

Researchers
Nick Menzies
Viktoria Schmitt
Steve Seigel

October 2006

About CSIS

The Center for Strategic and International Studies (CSIS) seeks to advance global security and prosperity in an era of economic and political transformation by providing strategic insights and practical policy solutions to decisionmakers. CSIS serves as a strategic planning partner for the government by conducting research and analysis and developing policy initiatives that look into the future and anticipate change. Our more than 25 programs are organized around three themes:

■ *Defense and Security Policy*—With one of the most comprehensive programs on U.S. defense policy and international security, CSIS proposes reforms to U.S. defense organization, defense policy, and the defense industrial and technology base. Other CSIS programs offer solutions to the challenges of proliferation, transnational terrorism, homeland security, and post-conflict reconstruction.

■ *Global Challenges*—With programs on demographics and population, energy security, global health, technology, and the international financial and economic system, CSIS addresses the new drivers of risk and opportunity on the world stage.

■ *Regional Transformation*—CSIS is the only institution of its kind with resident experts studying the transformation of all of the world's major geographic regions. CSIS specialists seek to anticipate changes in key countries and regions—from Africa to Asia, from Europe to Latin America, and from the Middle East to North America.

Founded in 1962 by David M. Abshire and Admiral Arleigh Burke, CSIS is a bipartisan, nonprofit organization headquartered in Washington, D.C., with more than 220 full-time staff and a large network of affiliated experts. Former U.S. senator Sam Nunn became chairman of the CSIS Board of Trustees in 1999, and John J. Hamre has led CSIS as its president and chief executive officer since 2000.

CSIS does not take specific policy positions; accordingly, all views expressed herein should be understood to be solely those of the author(s).

© 2006 by the Center for Strategic and International Studies. All rights reserved.

Cover photo: Archives of Jalalabad, Afghanistan. Photo by Dave Warner.

Library of Congress Cataloging-in-Publication Data
CIP information available upon request

Center for Strategic and International Studies
1800 K Street, N.W., Washington, D.C. 20006
Telephone: (202) 887-0200
Fax: (202) 775-3199
E-mail: books@csis.org
Web: www.csis.org/

Contents

Executive Summary

Collapsed and fragile states are now a focal point of foreign policy. During the past five years, such states have increasingly dominated the attention and resources of the U.S. government. Despite the importance of international interventions in conflict-prone settings, the record of success is mixed, and international actors struggle to establish minimum security and to reconstruct state institutions.

Persistent lack of success stems in part from problems of communication and connectivity between the diverse actors involved. More specifically, expertise gained from one international intervention does not adequately inform the next, and the wide array of international players lack an effective means of communicating with one another.

Recent technological innovations have fundamentally altered the information landscape just as developments in social network theory have changed how people connect and socialize. Taken together, these advancements have the potential to transform work in conflict-prone settings; however, they have not yet been fully incorporated into policy and practice.

Wikis, Webs, and Networks: Creating Connections for Conflict-Prone Settings recommends ways to improve connectivity between the various actors working in conflict-prone settings. The ultimate goal of enhanced connectivity is to enable local populations to prevent and mitigate conflict and help rebuild their country. This report is intended for civilians as well as the military, the public and private sectors, and Americans as well as international and national actors.

Four principles, proven true in a variety of settings and industries, form the basis of this report. If embraced, they have the potential to improve operations in conflict-prone settings.

- **Connectivity increases effectiveness.** Connectivity is the capacity for individuals and organizations to interface. Connectivity allows for, but does not guarantee, frequent and meaningful interactions, which can help diverse actors develop a common operating language, plan and conduct joint exercises, and integrate operations during crises.

- **Free revealing.** Openly sharing new ideas, innovations, and information is better suited to fast-paced, chaotic environments than is the traditional practice of closely managing information flows through established hierarchies.

- **Community generates content.** Relying on the community to generate, share, and interpret content makes the best use of resources and minimizes constraints in conflict settings. These settings demand flexibility and adaptability on many levels. User-driven content, in which all individuals contribute information, share con-

CSIS would like to acknowledge the support and assistance of the Office of the Assistant Secretary of Defense for Networks and Information Integration.

cepts, and evaluate resources, is the practical choice for environments with conflicting and unreliable data.

■ **Lead users drive the market.** By identifying and promoting the practices of lead users (those at the top end of the bell curve), the effectiveness of the entire international community can be enhanced.

Three strategic guidelines stem from these principles and provide a framework for enhancing connectivity in conflict-prone settings worldwide. These guidelines are not tied to any one tool or feature, but recommend ways for institutions to adjust and update policies, invest in appropriate communications infrastructure, and encourage cultural shifts.

■ Design architecture for participation

   • Expertise is not tied to individuals.

   • Contributions should be based on knowledge, not status or rank.

   • The participatory structure of networks is necessary to succeed in conflict-prone settings.

■ Strengthen social and knowledge networks

   • Communication is largely a social, not a technical, problem.

   • Incentives will encourage individuals to join communities.

   • Contributions will increase when individuals identify with the larger mission goals.

■ Use all available means of communication

   • Basic, commercially available means of communication are the most widely used.

   • Advanced technologies need to interface with common, low-tech tools.

   • Flexible tools that span no-tech to future-tech have the most value.

The Center for Strategic and International Studies (CSIS) recommends four implementation steps to make the above guidelines operational. These implementation points are low-cost, easy to apply, and catalytic for the longer process of transformation.

■ Create a consortium of implementing partners, universities, donors, and businesses to develop, promote, and implement the principles and strategic guidelines.

■ Sponsor pilot projects to test the effectiveness and operations of technology in the field. Open call centers with information, directory, and security hotlines. Distribute hand-held, durable, and cost-efficient communication tools to peacekeepers and local peacebuilders.

■ Build on successful Web sites and incorporate additional features. Market the Web sites across a range of communities.

- Conduct extensive outreach to promote the principles and raise awareness of the tools. Target entry pints to the four main communities; publicize and promote communities of practice.

CHAPTER I

The Problem

Introduction

The last two decades have brought revolutionary changes in the way security is defined and established: the consideration of collapsed and fragile states is now critical to U.S. foreign policy. There have been 34 international interventions in conflict-prone settings since 1989. Those that have occurred in the past five years have increasingly dominated the attention and resources of the U.S government and the dozens of countries involved in the operations of the United Nations (UN), European Union (EU), and North Atlantic Treaty Organization (NATO).[1] Nevertheless, international actors struggle to establish minimum security and to reconstruct state institutions.

During this same period, the number and types of actors on the ground have multiplied, while the challenges posed in these environments have become increasingly complex.[2] Foremost among these challenges are threats to people and societies that the U.S. Department of Defense (DOD), the UN, NATO, and others cannot contain. Smaller, more agile non-state entities have been able to outmaneuver dominant security and political institutions. Decentralized transnational terrorist networks and insurgencies have put chinks into the armor of industries that consume billions of dollars a year.[3]

Bureaucracies struggle to keep pace with the private sector and often lag behind in the adoption of new technologies and policies. A number of efforts, such as net-centric warfare, adopted by the U.S. military and other national or multinational actors, endeavor to make institutions more responsive to today's threats.[4] Despite significant progress, changes have not penetrated deeply or widely enough.[5] For U.S. and international institutions to "stay in the game," they need a better understanding of the

---

1. Charles Call, "*Institutionalizing Peace: A Review of Post-Conflict Peacebuilding Concepts and Issues for DPA*," United Nations Department of Political Affairs, January 31, 2005.

2. For example, see United Nations, "*A More Secure World: Our Shared Responsibility*" (Report of the Secretary-General's High-Level Panel on Threats Challenges and Change, 2005).

3. General Paul Van Riper defeated a $250 million war game, Millennium Challenge. For more information, see interview with Paul Van Riper, "Battle Plan Under Fire: The Immutable Nature of War," Public Broadcasting Service (PBS), December 17, 2003, http://www.pbs.org/wgbh/nova/wartech/nature.html.

4. See Clay Wilson, "*Network Centric Warfare: Background and Oversight Issues for Congress*" (Congressional Research Service report for Congress, June 2, 2004, p. 20).

changing technological and information landscape, particularly in international interventions.

In the last decade, international interventions have earned a mixed record at best. The moderate "successes" are disproportionate to the amount of money and number of lives that have been invested in conflict-prone environments.[6] Although the nature of the task is difficult, the UN, the United States, and allied partners must all do better.

The international community faces many constraints in conflict-prone settings: limited finances and personnel, inherently complex and difficult environments, and the urgent need to demonstrate positive results. To increase the likelihood of success, the numerous organizations working alongside one another must make use of their comparative advantages and work toward common goals, maximize the use of scarce resources, and ensure that investments have a multiplier effect. Individuals and organizations must also connect, communicate, and coordinate. If this occurs, former and ongoing international interventions will inform one another, and actors will have a higher degree of situational awareness.

A number of fields have capitalized on networks and new information technologies, including medicine, communications, and the media, in addition to private-sector businesses. Yet the humanitarian, development, security, and diplomatic communities lag far behind. This report recognizes that the sharing of information and expertise is a crucial element of success. Unfortunately it is an element not yet prioritized in doctrine and practice.

Wikis, Webs, and Networks: Creating Connections for Conflict-Prone Settings recommends ways to improve connectivity for the various actors working in these environments. This report is intended for civilians as well as the military, public as well as private sectors, and U.S. as well as international and other national actors. The goal of connectivity is to enable local populations to prevent and mitigate conflict and build peace.

This report proposes new ways to capitalize on all available resources to ensure effective information exchange among and between international and local actors, drawing on the strengths of practitioners, soldiers, and local populations as well as traditional post-conflict experts. Due to the diverse group of players and the dispersed nature of information and local knowledge in conflict-prone settings, these processes should be participatory, community-driven, and largely decentralized, and they should have buy-in from a diverse group of players.

The recommendations run counter to, and even threaten, traditional models of engagement in conflict-prone settings. Many players have a stake in maintaining the status quo—whether it is a rigid hierarchy, an overly proprietary information policy, or a marginalized local population. The importance of the task and the poor track record thus far mean that "business as usual" is no longer acceptable.

---

5. With the signing of the Department of Defense Directive 3000.05, Stability, Security, Transition, and Reconstruction (SSTR), operations were given the same priority as combat operations. To be effective, the military needs to ensure that the concepts of net-centric warfare extend to SSTR operations.

6. See James Dobbins et al., *America's Role in Nation-Building: From Germany to Iraq* (Santa Monica, Calif: RAND, 2003); James Dobbins et al., *The UN's Role in Nation-Building: From the Congo to Iraq* (Santa Monia: Calif: RAND, 2005).

This report is organized into four sections. The first defines the nature of the problem and examines the constraints associated with operating in conflict-prone settings. The second describes how recent trends in information sharing can improve results. The third section outlines four principles and provides strategic guidelines for enhancing connectivity. The fourth section prioritizes steps for implementation.

Nature of the Problem

More than one million soldiers and tens of thousands of civilians, whether led by U.S. or foreign governments, by the UN, or by other multilateral actors, have direct experience working in conflict-prone settings. Today, more players are involved than ever before, often with competing interests as well as different objectives, terminology, and information networks.

Two main problems relating to communication and connectivity plague reconstruction efforts:

■ The expertise gained from international interventions does not adequately inform other operations.

■ The actors, both international and local in a wide array, possess critical information but do not have an effective means of communicating with one another.

The terminology used to describe international interventions highlights discrepancies between the actors. The U.S. military alone has many different terms, including "peacekeeping and stability operations," "humanitarian assistance and disaster relief" (HADR), "security, stability, transition, and recovery operations" (SSTR), and "stability and reconstruction operations" (S&R). The U.S. Department of State created the Office of the Coordinator for Reconstruction and Stabilization(S/CRS), while the United Kingdom established the interdepartmental "Post-Conflict Reconstruction Unit." The UN refers to these operations as "integrated missions," but its Web site calls them "peacekeeping operations," and the broader concept is now encapsulated at the UN in the recently formed Peacebuilding Commission. Still others use the terms "conflict resolution" or "conflict transformation." All of these terms can refer to different activities, but many are used synonymously and interchangeably. The lack of common terminology is only one of many points of confusion among the PCRcommunity.[7]

Many segments within and between communities are reluctant or unable to share information, even though it could be critical to the work of the overall mission. Two anecdotes illustrate this point. The first concerns a U.S. Civil Affairs Marine officer in Falluja, Iraq.[8] He had access to Commander's Emergency Response (CERP) funds, but could not determine the best way to spend them: If the overarching goal was to revitalize the local economy, should he use the funds to buy tractors or seeds? Should he

---

7. For the purposes of this report, the terms "international intervention" and "conflict-prone setting" will be used to refer to all activities in countries in the midst of, emerging from, or descending into conflict.

8. This anecdote is only one of many CSIS heard during over a hundred interviews with practitioners who have recent experience in conflict-prone settings.

organize a farmer's cooperative? He was uncertain which course of action to take and did not know where to find the appropriate expertise or how to tap into it.

A second example concerns an international civilian conducting a health assessment of a rural area in Afghanistan. Available statistics were unreliable and outdated, and records of previous assessments were difficult to find. Other international organizations were working in the area, but there was no contact information for specific individuals. This aid worker conducted an assessment, collected information, and shared it with her organization. While her assessment may ultimately inform a country strategy, the process was long, cumbersome, and indirect.

How could the Marine have capitalized on the expertise of others? How could the aid worker have shared the results of her assessment with a broader audience, or how could she have found information from earlier and concurrent efforts? One could blame the Marine for not scouring hundreds of "lessons learned" reports on agricultural development, or his chain of command for not supporting him, or the development experts for not being stationed in Falluja, or indeed diplomatic security for not letting USAID move beyond security perimeters. Likewise, the aid worker in Afghanistan could also have trawled the Internet and files of organizations that might have conducted similar assessments.

These points may be true, but fundamentally, both anecdotes illustrate network problems. The network of the Marine in Falluja did not extend far enough to provide useful, timely advice. This was the case even though there were people working toward the same goals—although perhaps not in his unit or even in the military—who could have helped.

The case of the aid worker is different: she did not lack expertise – she lacked information. Data had been collected and compiled, but she did not have appropriate information networks to find it. There was no way to search or access the records of other assessments.

In both of these examples, individuals make decisions and duplicate past efforts without being able to access existing expertise and information. The negative impact of these decisions cannot be calculated, but it is significant.

In the case of the Marine, CERP funds are governed by the same principles as development assistance: outsiders injecting inputs into a community is a highly political action. In Iraq, CERP funds have been viewed by the U.S. government as "one of the primary tools for improving the lives of average Iraqi citizens" and are of utmost importance to the success of the reconstruction effort.[9] Giving money, for example, to this sheikh rather than that mayor or to this school instead of that health clinic, can have major ramifications for a community and how outsiders are perceived. Strike the wrong balance and well-intended aid can be counter-productive.[10] Similarly, numerous assessments that have no apparent payback tend to disillusion the local population who come to feel that their voices are ignored. At the national level, too many inefficiencies undermine an entire mission.

---

9. Brigadier General David N. Blackledge, "Coalition Provisional Authority Briefing," January 14, 2004, http://www.defenselink.mil/transcripts/2004/tr20040114-1144.html.

10. Peter Uvin, *Aiding Violence: The Development Enterprise in Rwanda* (West Hartford, Conn.: Kumarian Press, 1998).

Such situations have unfortunately been the norm rather than the exception in conflict-prone settings. Expertise exists, experiences have been accumulated, but they are not shared systematically and do not inform other cases adequately. Why does this continue to happen?

Operational Constraints

A number of constraints are present in each international intervention that contribute to the challenges facing actors and make information sharing and connectivity more difficult. These constraints can be grouped into the following four categories: 1) structural, 2) cultural, 3) environmental, and 4) technological. Each of these affects the way organizations and individuals connect, share information, and access expertise. Only when these challenges are understood and addressed can the international community improve its response to conflict on a global scale.

Structural Constraints

INSTITUTIONS ARE DISCONNECTED AND POLICIES ARE BURDENSOME. Institutions struggle to balance protecting sensitive information with sharing information that would be useful to partners. The traditional paradigm—that information is shared only on a "need-to-know" basis—has proved outdated.[11] In some cases, policies that aim to protect sensitive information can handicap the work of practitioners and undermine the entire reconstruction effort. Military personnel in Baghdad, for instance, regularly use three separate computers: one on a secret classified network, a second on a classified network, and a third on the open source Internet. Even unclassified documents cannot be easily shared if they are on the classified network, from which files can only be manually removed.

Prioritizing classified networks makes sense, but has the unintended consequence of making closed networks the de facto means of communication for those with access to them. As a result, NGOs, coalition partners, and contractors are excluded and cannot access information that would otherwise be useful to them. Some progress has been made to improve the sharing of classified information between government agencies. In many cases, however, information is not released or shared between organizations or within the U.S. government or UN agencies because it is marked as sensitive or official.[12]

The disconnect between local needs and the incentives for international organizations is a further structural constraint. Current incentives for organizations are based on funding: responsiveness to donors is rewarded more than success in meeting local needs. Donor procedures are demanding and time-consuming; however, even these checks and balances do not guarantee accountability. For example, one contractor may be awarded a tender to design a project and another one to implement it. This lack of

---

11. National Commission on Terrorist Attacks upon the United States, *The 9/11 Commission Report* (New York: Norton, 2004); *Creating a Trusted Network for Homeland Security: Second Report for the Markle Foundation Task Force*, 2003, http://www.markle.org/downloadable_assets/nstf_report2_full_report.pdf.

12. U.S. government agencies have numerous different ways to mark information as sensitive but unclassified. This makes sharing unclassified information between agencies difficult.

continuity and accountability can lead to project failure. Moreover, competition over funding and turf wars in a growing marketplace are additional barriers to improved collaboration.

Many successes are personality-driven and are hindered, rather than helped, by formal procedures. While some motivated individuals may work around institutional barriers, others are practically forced to disregard protocol. Outdated and overly strict policies often force individuals to break the rules for expediency and safety, a result that is in the interest neither of the individual nor of the organization, particularly when the aim of the overall exercise is to build accountable and transparent states.

Cultural Constraints

COMPETITION AND DIFFERING OBJECTIVES CONTRIBUTE TO LOW LEVELS OF TRUST. Many different cultures are present in international interventions. These include professional (e.g., humanitarian vs. military), geographic (international vs. national, international vs. international), temporal (long-term vs. short-term), ethnic, tribal, and religious. Organizations have contrasting objectives, strategies for reaching their goals, and measures of success, all of which contribute to misunderstanding and distrust. Even when actors overcome ideological, language, and professional barriers, other obstacles, such as competition over limited resources, remain.

Actors working in conflict-prone settings naturally cluster into groups, and these groups have competing objectives. The humanitarian, development, diplomatic, and security communities are highlighted here because individuals typically self-identify as part of these communities and they each have, for the most part, a common set of values and guiding principles.

Humanitarian organizations seek to prevent the immediate loss of life and secure basic needs, while attempting to abide by the principles of neutrality, impartiality, and independence. *Development* organizations are involved in a range of activities—from governance and rule of law to education and sanitation. They embrace values such as sustainability, capacity building, and local ownership.

These two approaches can come into conflict with one another during the transition from emergency relief to rehabilitation and recovery, particularly today with an expanded definition of humanitarianism.[13] This is often exacerbated when uniformed peacekeepers become involved in traditional humanitarian and development work in order to "win hearts and minds."

The *diplomatic* community's first duty is to their home country. Because they serve different functions, including acting as political representatives, military attaches, trade mission heads, and consular officers, there may be competing goals even within a mission. The *security* community comprises U.S. and foreign militaries, multilateral peacekeeping troops, international police, and private security companies. Missions can be at odds here too. Protecting diplomatic personnel and gaining the trust of the local population often conflict with one another.

Sharing information that may give "competitors" an edge is not usually part of organizational culture. Instead, protecting perceived "corporate interests" is the norm,

---

13. Randolph Kent et al., *The Future of Humanitarian Assistance: The Role of the United Nations* (New York: United Nations, 2004).

and is also a major reason why many coordination efforts fall flat.[14] As the oft-heard adage states, most people want to coordinate but no one wants to be coordinated.

If members of the international community are distrustful of one another, then local actors are even more distrustful of outsiders. The motives of an intervention and the amount of money involved can cause conflict. In some cases, internationals exacerbate the situation merely by their presence. In South Sudan, for instance, Muslim Bangladeshi troops were deployed even though many southern Sudanese equate Islam with the northern government and have consequently been wary of the Bangladeshi forces. Understandably, local actors are not confident that internationally installed systems will endure. Distrust of authority tends to pervade many post-conflict situations, and locals have uneven relations with international actors.

For effective results, the different communities must have not only the same destination in mind, but must also share a road map for getting there. Too often, these efforts have no way to integrate. The result is a stove-piped and incoherent strategy.[15]

Technological Constraints

LACK OF ACCESS AND INFRASTRUCTURE LIMIT TECHNOLOGY'S REACH.   Many actors lack consistent, reliable access to communications. Limited or no internet connectivity, sporadic or nonexistent cellular service, lack of power, and even bad transportation infrastructure make connecting on very basic levels impossible. Inefficient communication infrastructure can mean that something as simple as sending an email or setting up a meeting can prove extremely time-consuming.

When tools are available, training and maintenance pose another difficult element, as does the language barrier. Many communications tools are not sturdy enough for harsh conditions and frequently malfunction or break.

International organizations suffer from infrastructure issues as well. Bandwidth can be so limited as to be almost unusable; cellular service is uneven; and many headquarters staff rely so heavily on internet-based information that they effectively exclude colleagues working in more remote areas.

Interoperability—the ability of different systems to "talk" to each other—is a further obstacle. Incompatible radio systems, for instance, make civilian-to-military and even military-to-military communications difficult. Furthermore, organizations create their own databases, contact lists, and project updates without also investing in mechanisms for sharing that information. Occasionally, locals are not authorized to share communications tools despite having access, and hardware divisions mimic organizational divides.[16]

---

14. Anne Holohan, *Networks of Democracy: Lessons from Kosovo, for Afghanistan, Iraq, and Beyond* (Stanford, Calif.: Stanford University Press, 2005).

15. For a discussion of integration as it relates to U.S. national security, please see Michèle Flournoy and Shawn Brimley, "Strategic Planning for National Security: A New Project Solarium," *Joint Forces Quarterly* 42 (2006): 80–86.

16. In South Sudan, southern Sudanese soldiers were barred from using UN infrastructure such as Internet, despite being housed in the mission. Anne Holohan documents other instances of this in *Networks of Democracy*.

Environmental Constraints

INFORMATION IS IMPERFECT AND IMPROVISATION IS INEVITABLE. Conflict-prone settings tend to have scant, unreliable, and contradictory information as well as out-of-date (or nonexistent) statistics. These difficulties are compounded by security concerns and lack of infrastructure, which hampers the collection of new information. For instance, estimates of the population of Somalia range from 6 to 10 million, and despite the publication of widespread "statistics" on Afghanistan, the last national census was conducted in 1979. Estimates of displaced persons in Darfur, or Iraqi civilian casualties, differ by the tens of thousands.

The numbers used can seem like little more than guesswork and, accordingly, claims of success or failure are difficult to separate from political spin. In such an environment, rumors easily take hold and are hard to disprove. The lack of data directly affects the ability of practitioners, including soldiers and even intelligence analysts, to make well-informed decisions, which depend on a full understanding of the context and situation on the ground.

Further, organizations also suffer from high staff turnover, inadequate numbers of personnel, and lack of staff with the right expertise. High staff turnover means that practitioners who have learned about local conditions are replaced by novices. New staff may overlap with their immediate predecessor (although this is rare), but seldom do they connect with employees from earlier rotations.

Practitioners have limited time and a surfeit of information. They are confronted with, paradoxically, too much information but limited situational awareness due to low-quality, irrelevant, or sanitized information. Practitioners cope with rapidly changing environments, uncertainty, system failure, and revisions of work plans and responsibilities. Everyone must make do in less than ideal circumstances, with inadequate resources. Training can help prepare practitioners for these environments, but improvisation and flexibility are essential.

CHAPTER 2

The Possibilities

Networks, Hierarchies, and Expertise

The constraints discussed do not doom all interventions to failure, but they present challenges to individuals working in conflict-prone environments. This section will look at ways to help overcome these challenges and improve outcomes. It will suggest ways that new trends in information sharing and network theory can be adapted to conflict-prone settings.

The term "network" refers to many different types of relationships, from social to technological. This report uses the term broadly to describe connections between people and organizations and to encompass the defining characteristics of networks: flexibility, responsiveness, and interdependence of actors.[17]

Organizations traditionally rely on hierarchies as a way of ensuring a clear division of labor, lines of authority, and accountability. In turbulent or chaotic conflict-prone settings, however, organizations need to be more flexible. In contrast to hierarchies, networks allow information to flow both vertically and horizontally. These information flows permit direct exchange between practitioners and decrease the inefficiencies that arise when working only through established lines of authority.

How can social, professional, and information networks help governmental and non-governmental actors work together to produce a more agile and locally rooted response? Can changes be made within organizations that lower the transaction cost of coordination?

Organizational changes can be made without disrupting traditional lines of authority, and at the same time, can empower employees to make timely decisions. The Toyota Production System is an instructive example of employees working together in a collaborative fashion within an established hierarchy.[18] Toyota has promoted a shared pool of knowledge and universally available tools for moving knowledge around the organization, as part of a new set of work, communication, and leadership practices. Instead of relying on formal processes for resolving problems, employees can solve them in informal, spontaneous, and collaborative ways. This type of flexibility and behavior

---

17. See Anne Holohan's *Networks of Democracy.* Patrice C. McMahon, *Taming Ethnic Hatred: Ethnic Cooperation and Transnational Networks in Eastern Europe* (Syracuse, N.Y.: Syracuse University Press, forthcoming).

18. Philip Evans and Bob Wolf, "Collaboration Rules," *Harvard Business Review* (July 2005): 96.

maximizes the strengths of the new technological tools and takes the changing operating environment into account.

Communities of Practice (CoPs), sometimes called networks of practice, provide a way to enhance social learning by means of networks. CoPs are made up of groups of professionals who share information and advice on a particular topic to solve problems. CoPs can take the form of training seminars, conference series, listservs, and Web sites, and extend beyond the bounds of traditional hierarchies. Members of a certain rank or position can focus on specific issues that they face in common.

Networks that enable lateral connections improve effectiveness within hierarchical organizations. CompanyCommand, a Web site started by two U.S. Army captains who recognized the utility in sharing information with their peer group, is an excellent example of this.[19] Although the Center for Army Lessons Learned (CALL) collected and disseminated official lessons learned, CALL had its limits, relying on field anecdotes and experiences being processed up through the bureaucracy and translated into doctrine. The lessons were then sent back to the operators, in an elongated feedback loop. CompanyCommand enables Captains to share first-hand tactical experiences—person to person in real time—more efficiently than any formal process could.[20]

Networks are also suited to improved collaboration between independent hierarchies working alongside one another.[21] Boundaries between organizations become more permeable if the broad goals of a mission are promoted and new technologies are harnessed. This has been documented in two municipalities in Kosovo.[22] The UN-run municipality with a more networked structure was more effective than the traditionally hierarchical municipality, despite similar conditions in each. The two municipal administrators differed in their approach to interpreting the UN's mandate, understanding collaboration, and implementing information sharing. The more successful administrator had a military background while his deputy had a business background. They understood roles and responsibilities broadly, and sought out connections with locals. Together, they encouraged employees to share information, collaborate with other international organizations and include locals in decision-making. The second administrator viewed his mandate narrowly and did not see collaboration as essential to the mission.

When a practitioner identifies with a broader goal than her job description alone, she is more willing to contribute and assist others in their work. Voluntary cooperation reduces delays, solves problems, and lowers the transaction cost of collaboration. Networks with a high degree of trust enable information exchange between otherwise disparate actors. These networks both harness collective intelligence and draw on the specialized knowledge of experts.[23]

---

19. The original site address was http://www.companycommand.com. The Army has since recognized the utility of the site and now hosts and sponsors it at: http://companycommand.army.mil.

20. For more information see Dan Baum, "Battle Lessons: What the Generals Don't Know," *New Yorker*, January 17, 3005.

21. Anne Holohan, *Networks of Democracy*.

22. Ibid.

23. Tim O'Reilly quoted by Steven Levy and Brad Stone, "The New Wisdom of the Web," *Newsweek*, April 3, 2006, p. 49.

Expertise of a few and the "collective intelligence" of many can co-exist. In some situations, a certain expertise is needed, while in others, basic information is sufficient. Information and expertise are complementary, as increased data means more raw material for analysis. Although the intelligence community, among others, has increasingly recognized the value of open source information, gathering information from all possible sources is a long way off.[24]

Comparing professional photographers and lay contributors to an online photo-sharing site demonstrates the strengths of cultivating both expertise and raw data. National Geographic photographers have a refined skill, much like post-conflict experts. In contrast, contributors to Flickr, an online photo-sharing Web site, are not professionals and do not have the same skill level. They do, however, post millions of images for the world to see. Because anyone can contribute, vast quantities of information become available.

The international community relies heavily on the equivalent of the professional photographer: intelligence analysts, assessment teams, and professional pollsters. The problem is not in the experts, but rather in the absence of systematic ways for the generalist to contribute. More contributions will increase both the amount of information and the speed at which the information is shared. Now, it is common for the first photos of news events to appear on Flickr before they are published by news agencies, as occurred after the 2004 bombing of the Australian Embassy in Jakarta.[25]

More broadly, recent technological advances have fundamentally altered the information landscape. These have revolutionized business and politics, created new industries, and forced others to adapt to keep pace. Many of these advances could be particularly useful for conflict-prone settings.

Trends in Information Sharing

This section examines the applicability of three new trends to conflict-prone settings: online social networking, wikis, and tagging. The features themselves are secondary to the changes—conceptual and practical—they make possible.

Online Social Networking

Online social networking is a new and expanding trend, and the proliferation of sites such as MySpace, LinkedIn, and Facebook demonstrate their immense popularity. MySpace has at times received more hits than Google, including 760,000 new users in one day.[26] Social networking has changed the traditional view of the Internet as primarily a means to access information (like a library), to a participatory, community-like network. Social networking allows users to access information and also to access people.

---

24. See Richard A. Brest, Jr., "Intelligence Issues for Congress," Congressional Research Service Issue Brief for Congress, May 9, 2006.

25. Ibid. CNN had become one of the quickest sources of useful information on current events in recent years. Now even this news source is not as quick as Flickr.

26. Levy and Stone, "The New Wisdom of the Web."

Social networking, and the ways in which users can categorize themselves and link to other users, allows for easy searching of people, the creation of effective networks, and the sharing of relevant information and expertise. In sites such as Friendster, a user can create a visible social network, in which he is able to see the friends of his friends. By doing so, he finds and connects with people who are not in his immediate group of friends. For instance, someone moving to a new city where he does not know anyone could search his extended social network to find friends of friends who live there. This has always happened informally: friends ask one another if they know of anyone living in a given city or with a particular interest. Friendster and other social networking sites enhance and improve this process.

The same feature would be immensely helpful to the universe of players in conflict-prone settings. Professional networks, which now exist mostly on informal levels, could become easily searchable. Even though each conflict-prone setting is unique, many have common needs, such as establishing transitional justice mechanisms. At present, the lessons from one location are not systematically used for the benefit of another. New technologies means that rather than asking colleagues for suggestions of someone with experience in setting up, for example, human rights commissions, one could search the network until finding the appropriate person. This would also reduce spam, as requests would target only a small group of people with relevant skills and experience.

The social premise of such networks means that people willingly and actively join and contribute. Once the network reaches its tipping point, with a sufficient number of active users, it becomes a magnet and the place where everyone goes.[27] Combining social and professional elements creates additional incentives to join and participate.

Wikis

Collaborative Web sites or software, called wikis, allow users to add and edit content. By providing an alternative to established authorities, wikis have changed the way in which information and expertise is conceived of and used. For instance, the *Encyclopedia Britannica* has traditionally been the best resource for a readily available explanation on, for example, the causes, characteristics, and history of tsunamis. The main barriers to accessing this information were the cost of the publication (derived from the necessity of staffing researchers) and the few minutes it took to locate the entry in the correct volume. The limitations were threefold: entries were only updated on an annual basis; content was not subject to review beyond a narrow circle of experts; and the organizational scheme was predefined.

Today, a new resource, *Wikipedia*, has emerged. The content provided by *Wikipedia* is determined by users themselves and provided free and instantaneously to anyone with an Internet connection. Entries are continually updated, so, for example, maps of devastation wrought by the Asian tsunami on December 26, 2004, did not have to wait until the 2006 edition to be published. Although early submissions may be erroneous or incomplete, the principle that governs *Wikipedia* is that "anyone can edit," and any-

---

27. Malcolm Gladwell, *The Tipping Point: How Little Things Can Make a Big Difference* (Boston, Mass.: Back Bay Books, 2002).

thing can be improved. Over time, to the surprise of many, the "wisdom of the crowd" consistently proves more astute than small groups of esteemed experts.[28]

Wikipedia and the *Encyclopedia Britannica* have a similar, but not overlapping, purpose. Comparisons between them, while instructive, overlook the core strengths of each.[29] Published encyclopedias are meant to be authoritative, with validated and reliable information. Expertise and trustworthiness, rather than timeliness, provide utility for the reader. *Wikipedia's* strength, on the other hand, is the ability to define emergent categories: events, concepts, or individuals that become important or noteworthy overnight. Hurricane Katrina, politicians, and trends are outside of the scope of traditional encyclopedias. Rather than relying on a set of predetermined experts, *Wikipedia* relies on anyone who has information to add.

The notion that "anyone can edit" is radical for institutions that go to great lengths to limit who has access to content, let alone who is allowed to generate it. There is a difference, however, between limiting access to plans and operations, and limiting access to knowledge that increases the effectiveness of operations and programs. Experts and senior leaders have a vital role to play in determining mission success or failure, but their reach or understanding of the fluid situation on the ground may be different depending on where they sit. It is often left to the field staff—whether soldiers, diplomats, or humanitarian or development actors—to interpret, analyze, and improvise in a fast-moving environment.

Information is now available in real-time and generated by people who need not know each other or have geographic proximity. The ease of compilation makes more customized information available, and the flexibility of the tool accommodates both instant alerts and long-running debates. For instance, residents of Kabul can add online updates about the location of riots, and with the same tool academics can engage in in-depth debates about how best to address spoilers.

Tagging

"Tagging" is a third example of a trend that has altered how users engage with information. Users can mark a piece of data with any number of keywords (tags). These tags are then used by others to search for, and identify, pieces of information. Unlike libraries, which must file books and articles according to one categorization system (be it the Library of Congress or the Dewey Decimal System), tagging allows for new categories to continually emerge and for users to fit information into their own organizational scheme. An unlimited number of identifiers can mark reports: an article does not have to be catalogued as either about Liberia or civil society development. Users can identify the report with words that indicate its utility to them.

Tagging can help highlight the best resources and filter out irrelevant information. Sites like *Del.icio.us* let users bookmark Web sites they find interesting and makes these

---

28. James Surowiecki, *The Wisdom of Crowds: Why the Many Are Smarter Than the Few and How Collective Wisdom Shapes Business, Economies, Societies and Nations* (New York: Doubleday, 2004).

29. Jim Giles, "Internet Encyclopedias Go Head to Head," *Nature* 438 (December 15, 2005): 900-901; also see *Encyclopaedia Britannica*, "Fatally Flawed: Refuting the Recent Study on Encyclopedic Accuracy in the Journal *Nature*," March 2006, http://corporate.britannica.com/britannica_nature_ response.pdf; and *Nature*, "*Encyclopedia Britannica* and *Nature*: A Response," March 2006, http://www.nature.com/nature/britannica/index.html.

bookmarks public.[30] This can be useful in two ways: users can search through what others have "tagged" with certain terms; and users can see which words others used to tag the same item. If someone searches for the tag "Kosovo," she can see what Web sites and documents users thought were valuable enough to save and mark. This is more helpful than an Internet search because typically casual readers will not tag sites they are only browsing. Instead, the most valuable resources that Kosovo-followers have marked show up, filtering the mass of information.

The second feature helps to clarify terminology issues. If a user finds a Web site useful and marks it as "peacekeeping," he can see that others have labeled the same Web site with the words "peacebuilding," "relief," "recovery," or "PCR." He may then want to look for resources with these different terms—as the broad user community has grouped the terms together.

These three examples are just some of the new technologies that have created possibilities that could hardly be imagined only five years ago and go a long way toward transforming and improving information sharing. To make the best use of these tools, organizations will need to adapt to a different information landscape. Who generates information, who uses information, and the levels of verification and timeliness required have all changed.

Limitations

The capacity to connect is essential if international and local actors seek to incorporate the features mentioned above. It is also true, however, that connectivity alone will not produce better results. Actors may still fail to coordinate because organizations are unwilling to modify and harmonize their objectives. Competition exists between individuals, organizations, and communities, not least for funding and accolades. Connected actors may continue to hold their cards close to their chest or talk past each other, while important actors may be left out of the room entirely.

When institutions are reluctant to coordinate or share information, enabling individuals to do so is an alternative. People are often willing to work around institutional boundaries if they know and trust staff from other institutions, ultimately helping to mitigate overall competition between organizations.

Reluctance to coordinate is one obstacle; institutional and individual resistance to information sharing is another. This opposition stems from reasonable concerns. The highest standards of data verification and security aim to save lives and protect systems from sabotage. Yet situations vary, and "pre-vetted" information can be as valuable as verified information in many cases.

For example, when information cannot be formally verified, sheer quantity, rather than strict oversight, enables self-regulation. Any one piece of information can be confirmed, or refuted, by other accounts—something that relying on only a handful of intelligence analysts does not allow.

In other instances, user-driven reviews on sites such as Amazon.com can be manipulated for self-promotion or partisan criticism. Although these open systems are

---

30. Delicious, http://del.icio.us, is the dominant site that allows users to share online bookmarks.

vulnerable to sabotage, in practice they have largely proven to self-correct and minimal regulations can go a long way towards preventing misuse.[31] Basic policies can reduce, though not eliminate, this risk while retaining the value of the feature. In addition, in many cases, the daily benefits of open information systems outweigh the potential threats.[32]

---

31. Despite some high-profile cases of misinformation on *Wikipedia*, the vast majority of entries are self-corrected in short amounts of time. The utility of the information proves of overwhelming value when compared to the small chance of risk. See Katie Hafner, "Growing *Wikipedia* Refines Its 'Anyone Can Edit' Policy," *New York Times,* June 17, 2006, A1.

32. http://www.amazon.com now has ways to discriminate among reviewers, with "badges" such as Top 10 reviewer and name certification.

The Strategy

This report is guided by a view that connectivity will be a catalyst for better results. The majority of players, local and international, are already committed to the wider goals of the mission—as evidenced by their participation in often risky operations—yet lack the means to achieve their goals as effectively as they could. Providing basic tools and improving connectivity will enable innovations to flourish, and practitioners to accomplish the difficult tasks of reconstruction.

This section presents four principles that form the foundation of this report. Based on these principles, CSIS devised three strategic guidelines to provide a framework for enhancing connectivity in conflict-prone settings across the globe.

Principles

The PCR Project examined theories and innovations from a wide range of fields to determine their applicability to policy and practice in conflict-prone environments. Studies by network theorists, social scientists, and other researchers were examined in light of the expertise and experience of the PCR Project's staff and its Board of Advisers. From these fields, four principles have been drawn that form the theoretical basis for improving communication and effectiveness. These principles have proven themselves true in a variety of industries and settings. If embraced, they have the potential to improve operations in conflict-prone settings.

Connectivity Increases Effectiveness

Connectivity is the capacity of individuals and organizations to interface with each other. Frequent and meaningful interactions can help diverse actors develop a common operating language, plan and conduct joint exercises, and integrate operations during crises.

A high degree of connectivity lends itself to a densely interconnected network. In such a network, "there is more power in being an information source than an information sink" and information is more likely to be shared than hoarded.[33] The strength of the network ensures that information will find its way around any bottlenecks and

---

33. Evans and Wolf, "Collaboration Rules."

choke points.[34] Being a source of information brings benefits, increasing the visibility and influence of the provider.

Free Revealing Makes Sense

A second principle guiding this report is that "free revealing" is better suited to fast-paced, chaotic environments than the traditional practice of closely managing information flows through established hierarchies. Simply put, free revealing is openly sharing new ideas and innovations, and it accounts for the success of those who share ideas that traditionally would have been considered proprietary.[35] There has been a surge of new ideas, innovations, and even technical solutions that have hit the marketplace free of charge—with the owners making a profit from being the first to have the idea, rather than from being the only one. The success of online communities such as Company-Command, user-driven sites such as *Wikipedia*, and open-source coding such as Linux all demonstrate that this new way of viewing information—as a public commodity—is taking hold.

In many ways, free revealing is the antithesis of the way governments, militaries, and businesses typically function. Relinquishing control over content is perceived by many to endanger U.S. interests and personnel, undermine orders from superiors and the wisdom of experts, diminish the power that comes from holding on to knowledge, and open institutions to criticism as the limits of their knowledge are revealed. Because traditional ways of managing information flows are becoming counter-productive, free revealing must find a way to work within the context of institutional realities.

Community Generates Content

Relying on the community to generate, share, and interpret content makes the best use of resources and minimizes constraints in conflict settings. These settings demand flexibility and adaptability on many levels. User-driven content, in which all individuals contribute information, share concepts, and evaluate resources, is the practical choice for fast-paced environments with conflicting and unreliable data. Indeed, large amounts of rapidly changing data can quickly overwhelm centrally managed systems.

In many cases, users have the most up-to-date and detailed information. "Mash-ups," in which users add commentary and information to, for example, an online map, are a good example. After Hurricane Katrina, users posted information about the status of the flooding or details of damage to houses on maps provided by Mapquest and Googlemaps. In Baghdad, detailed information about violence in each area of the city has been added to freely available maps.

Further, systems with rigid architectures cannot always incorporate uses other than that for which they were intended. Something as basic as online registration forms with only a set number of fields, such as name, organization, and topic of interest, can be constraining; developers have to foresee every possible field users could want. A flexible structure, however, would allow users to add new fields as the need arose. A user might

---

34. Duncan Watts, "Decentralized Intelligence: What Toyota Can Teach the 9/11 Commission about Intelligence Gathering," *Slate*, August 5, 2004.

35. Principle I and Principle IV were derived from the work of Eric von Hippel, *Democratizing Innovation* (Cambridge, Mass.: MIT Press, 2005).

wish to share her regional interest—and could add that category if the system has been designed with user-driven content in mind.

Encouraging users to generate, structure, and evaluate content makes the most of their insights. There are numerous experts with content to share—as well as many practitioners who may have smaller, but still insightful, success stories from their experience on the ground. Furthermore, practitioners are very willing to share their experiences; they do not lack the will to help, only the means to do so. Even if only a small fraction of the millions of people who have experience with international interventions are able to share their ideas, then a huge increase in knowledge and understanding is possible.

Lead Users Drive the Market

Finally, this report is guided by a view that "lead users" drive the market. The private sector research and development industry has increasingly come to rely on a group known as "lead users"—selected customers who develop new products by adapting existing ones to fit their needs.[36] A lead user is any individual or organization that best utilizes resources, irrespective of their position in a hierarchy or their formal job title. As a result of their innovation, new, original, and unforeseen uses for products are developed. These uses are initially adapted by those on the fringe, but in time they often become mainstream practice.

The "lead user" model fits well with the theory that policymakers and practitioners fall along a bell curve. A small percentage is quite good and attuned to the strategic choices facing local actors. They are knowledgeable of the particular history, culture, and politics of the place, and experienced with political transitions, including rebuilding fragile states and war-torn societies. A small percentage of policymakers are also dangerously bad, routinely falling into well-known and avoidable traps. The majority, however, falls somewhere in between these two poles—in the middle of the bell curve. By identifying and promoting the practices of lead users (those at the top end of the bell-curve), the effectiveness of the entire international community can be enhanced.

These principles are not a common feature of the literature on conflict-prone settings. Yet it is clear that thinking from other fields can be incorporated into the discourse. Ideas about organizational management and the distribution of innovations have important implications for how the international community undertakes work in conflict-prone settings. Organizational design, collection, and use of information, and mechanisms for coordination are essential to meeting the goals of the intervention and ultimately achieving better results.

Strategic Guidelines

Three strategic guidelines provide a vision for the design of new information systems and structures. Because technologies develop at such a rapid pace, the following recommendations are not tied to any one tool or feature. Instead, they provide a framework for institutions to adjust and update policies, invest in appropriate communications infrastructure, and encourage cultural shifts. They are also aimed at individuals who

---

36. von Hippel, *Democratizing Innovation*.

can, by collective behavior, force institutions to take notice of the changing environment. By combining a top-down and bottom-up approach, change will be most likely to transform the operating environment and community.

Design Architecture of Participation

- Expertise is not tied to individuals.

- Contribution should be based on knowledge, not status or rank.

- The participatory structure of networks is necessary to succeed in conflict-prone settings.

The complex nature of post-conflict settings guarantees that information is not limited to a finite number of people. Instead, individuals and organizations (both local and international) have different types of expertise. Participatory systems and structures would make the best use of each person's knowledge and ensure maximum situational awareness for all actors.

An "architecture of participation" describes systems with low barriers to entry that are designed for openness and user contribution. These systems are characterized by free information flows, which reinforce transparency and self-regulation. A participatory structure will not undermine hierarchies so much as elevate valuable contributors, who are evaluated on merit, rather than position and title.

Innovations need not be formally collected in a lessons-learned process or originate only from a central headquarters: they can come from anywhere. The more available the data, the better the community can evaluate the utility of contributions and separate the insights from the "noise." If more information is categorized and differentiated by the community, it will mitigate information overload. Allowing innovations to hit the marketplace as and when they are developed will start the process of building a community consensus on good ideas and improving the quality of dialogue.

Participatory structures that foster engagement and local contribution mimic the participatory nature of democracies—a central goal of international intervention.

Strengthen Social and Knowledge Networks

- Communication is largely a social, not a technical, problem.

- Incentives will encourage individuals to join communities.

- Contributions will increase when individuals identify with the larger mission goals.

Social networks built on trust and personal relationships provide a sense of community, identity, and commonality. In turn, these networks facilitate information sharing. Individuals will collaborate, solve problems, and offer themselves as a resource when they identify with a community.

For information to flow across community divides, members must identify with a mission larger than their organization's own goals. In places where trust is a rare commodity, personal relationships are essential for making things happen. Actors must also recognize that while there may be different, and in some cases, competing, tactical objectives, all can derive mutual benefit from cooperation. Despite different cultures, ideological arguments can be overcome when people work together on a concrete problem, form personal relationships, and develop trust. Broader ideological issues can be broken down at a person-to-person level.

To develop a successful community, incentives should entice members to participate and keep them actively engaged. Low barriers to entry and a stimulating vision or mission are appropriate incentives for participation. A strong group identity and social pressure—often in a small group setting—encourages sustained commitment.[37] Informal social gatherings are an essential way to build trust between international actors and locals.

Incentives that appeal to social needs can be especially effective. Social connections provide a foundation for trust, which can then facilitate professional information sharing. Cooperation on even non-work-related issues often increases the capacity for individuals to work together.[38]

Use All Available Means of Communication

- Basic, commercially available means of communication are the most widely used.

- Advanced technologies need to interface with common, low-tech tools.

- Flexible tools that span no-tech to future-tech have the most value.

Solutions for enhancing information sharing must span the range of technical capabilities—from lowest-common denominator tools, such as cell phones and commercial emails, to developing technologies that have not yet hit the marketplace. These technologies should be able to interface with one another easily. For the high-tech to be useful, a village cell phone needs to link to a high-power computer. Interoperability and ubiquity (the widespread availability of technology) are mandatory for maximizing current capabilities and addressing future needs.

If technology is too advanced for the local infrastructure, its utility diminishes and it becomes exclusive, as not all actors have equivalent capabilities. Still, advanced technology has enormous value for practitioners, providing imagery and situational awareness that far exceeds what has been available in the past. Technologically advanced tools and features such as maps and GIS data, imagery, and collaborative software are invaluable and can enhance situational awareness for all actors.[39] Their use should be encouraged, as should the ability to interface with other more basic technology.

Increasing access to these tools will provide a high payoff in terms of connectivity. Currently, too many locals are cut off and unable to rely on the infrastructure that expatriates import, often only for their own use. Providing a host nation's people with a degree of connectivity will develop trust, foster partnership, and build local capacity.[40]

---

37. Malcolm Gladwell, "The Cellular Church: How Rick Warren Built His Ministry," *New Yorker*, September 12, 2005.

38. This has been documented in examples such as the game ScudHunt, which builds trust and facilitates collaboration in other activities, developed by ThoughtLink. Presentation by Julia Loughran, "Institutional Issues and Innovative Solutions for Bringing People Together," National Defense University, April 27, 2006.

39. Such as Sharepoint and Groove.

Policies, habits, and technology use will not change overnight. It is unwise to wait for every classification issue to be untangled and every cultural difference to be overcome before implementing reforms. Instead, solutions should target those who need and want better tools. Empowering those who want change will push up the bell curve and improve practices community wide.

40. Many local communities have already discovered the benefits of Internet connectivity. Rebel groups communicate via blogs and Web sites. See Emily Wax, "African Rebels Take Their Battles Online: Internet Extends Political Debate," *Washington Post*, January 14, 2006, p. A16.

CHAPTER 4

The Solution

Implementation

This section details the priority implementation steps that will accelerate the pace with which the international community incorporates technological and cultural changes to increase connectivity. They provide actionable ways to make systems more user-driven, create incentives for participation, and link up high and low-tech methods of communications to reach the largest possible audience. Additionally, the implementation steps are inexpensive, easy to apply, and catalytic to the longer process of transformation.

The four recommendations are: 1) create a consortium to initiate implementation of the principles and strategic guidelines; 2) undertake pilot projects to test the applicability of technologies to conflict-prone settings; 3) build on successful Web sites by incorporating additional features; and 4) conduct extensive outreach to promote and expand the impact of the principles and strategic guidelines. These four areas of focus are interconnected; progress in one area is likely to bolster outcomes in the others, as each increases the overall connectivity of actors in conflict-prone settings.

Create a Consortium

CSIS recommends developing a consortium of organizations with a high-level of interest in sharing and promoting the principles and strategic guidelines and beginning their implementation. A diverse and committed group of practitioners, policymakers, academics, and businesspeople, representing the private and public sectors, is vital to implementing the ideas expressed in this report. An international consortium has the potential to generate worldwide interest and make real change. An integrated group would be able to promote an integrated response. This "top-down" approach should influence key actors' perspectives on the enormous importance of information exchange across communities in the post-conflict reconstruction arena.

A highly involved group with a vested interest in the issue would be an invaluable asset in implementing this report's recommendations. Sustained involvement would provide a guiding strategic vision and ensure that efforts at coordination and connectivity are not simply "one-offs" that have no long-term impact. This group would be instrumental in alerting the wide array of actors to the value of the principles and strategic guidelines.

Dozens of organizations have been consulted in the course of preparing this report. In addition, CSIS created a Board of Advisers whose members have been involved throughout the life of the project.[41] A number of organizations have already committed to continued involvement and collaboration on implementing recommendations. The consortium, which is poised to move ahead, would generate momentum to transform what is now purely conceptual into policy and action.

The consortium should undertake a number of activities, such as implementing recommendations in their own organizations, designing pilot projects, convening conferences and roundtables, generating interest among donor countries, and sponsoring training exercises.

Convening conferences

The strategic partnerships in the consortium would create a forum for ongoing, high-level dialogue. Frequent conferences and roundtables would encourage feedback and further develop the principles and strategic guidelines.

Consortium members could also reach out to practitioners by delivering presentations at training centers, and holding seminars with experienced practitioners. CSIS recommends sponsoring several "cross-community" conferences to foster face-to-face information sharing, and build enthusiasm for free-revealing, information sharing, and developing trust. This would also be used to develop a community of reachback experts and consultants from these organizations who could be reached at any time to offer advice.

Partnering with donor countries

The consortium should co-host meetings with donor countries and multilateral organizations to generate interest and involvement. The following donor countries and multilateral organizations should be targeted: Asian Development Bank, Australia, Canada, Denmark, European Union, Germany, Inter-American Development Bank, Japan, Millennium Challenge Corporation, Norway, Organization for Economic Cooperation and Development (OECD), Organization for Security and Cooperation in Europe (OSCE), Sweden, UN, United Kingdom, and World Bank.

Sponsor training exercises

The consortium could also sponsor training exercises as an effective means of breaking down walls prior to and during interventions. Personal relationships facilitate collaboration and an organizing group can mobilize involvement. Exercises such as Strong Angel, a project that brings together staff from many organizations, help to build these types of relationships.[42]

Conduct Pilot Projects

A prototype program or policy with demonstrated success would build momentum for widespread change. CSIS recommends undertaking a number of pilot projects that experiment with the easiest, most cost-efficient, and most effective ways to connect internationals and locals to one another. Case studies that demonstrate the utility of enhanced connectivity in the field should promote investment in communications

---

41. A list of board members is attached in appendix 4.
42. For more information, see http://www.strongangel3.org.

resources. Successes, and even partial failures, would better inform policies and future interventions.

The following pilot projects would facilitate interface between low-tech and high-tech. These pilots could provide concrete results and illustrate the impact of connectivity on effectiveness. They could also be used as a comparison to determine the highest-value and lowest-cost options.[43]

OPEN CALL CENTERS WITH INFORMATION, DIRECTORY, AND SECURITY HOT-LINES. Cellular networks have been exceptionally successful in a number of post-conflict and developing countries. In Afghanistan, for instance, locals and internationals rely on them as the primary means of communication in much of the country. With such widespread use, phones can be better used to help practitioners in the field and individuals involved in reconstruction and capacity-building efforts to get the information they need.[44] Opening up a call center would increase the utility of this widely available means of communication.

CSIS recommends that the international community support central hotlines to expand the existing capability of phone networks, allowing experts to provide detailed advice to callers or redirect them to an individual or organization able to help. This capability can be expanded even further if users are able to connect to the hotline through the Internet or via Skype.

Staffing a call center 24 hours a day, 7 days a week in a capital city such as Kabul would have limited cost and multiplier effects. The value of citywide central hotlines has been confirmed across the United States and notably in New York, where three central numbers with different functions—311, 411, and 911—are able to help a wide range of citizens solve their problems.[45] While 911 handles emergencies and security issues, and 411 provides directory information, the less conventional 311 hotline created in 2003 has found success as a center point for New Yorkers to report "non-emergency" problems and receive advice.

A 311 hotline would allow international and local staff to reach an information call center. Operators would inform callers of road closings and planned demonstrations, and provide alternative routes. Experts could be on call to answer technical questions in

---

43. For more information on communications tools that are appropriate to a range of settings see, Frank Kramer, "In the Eye of the Storm: A Primer on ICT Support for Civil-Military Coordination in Stabilization & Reconstruction and Disaster Relief Operations," National Defense University, Discussion Draft, October 27, 2005, http://www.ndu.edu/CTNSP/S&RWorkshop_Oct05/ICT%20SR%20Primer%20(discussion%20draft).doc, and Larry Wentz, "Information and Communication Technologies for Civil-Military Coordination in Disaster Relief and Stabilization and Reconstruction," Center for Technology and National Security Policy, National Defense University, July 2006, http://www.ndu.edu/ctnsp/Def_Tech/DTP31%20ICT%20Primer.pdf.

44. Some invaluable information dissemination services already exist: the Afghanistan Information Management Service (AIMS), a venture by the UNOCHA and UNDP, has been working to develop capacity in "information management systems," providing GIS, database, and information coordination training to government staff and other organizations. The Afghan Research and Evaluation Unit (AREU) aims to provide reliable data and analysis on Afghan issues, and the Afghanistan NGO Security Office (ANSO) coordinates security efforts for NGOs. These programs have helped with information organization and coordination, but in many cases do not increase the size of the network that individual practitioners and Afghans have to solve problems as they arise.

45. Winnie Hu, "City's 311 Line Takes Big Step Past Potholes," *New York Times*, July 19, 2004, B1.

real time and respond to information requests. This hotline would greatly simplify the information-search process by providing a central location for individuals involved in post-conflict reconstruction across all communities in Kabul to speak to the relevant expert and quickly receive the information they need.

The 311 number has been successful in urban environments with widespread communications infrastructure. In post-conflict environments, with a much lower infrastructure baseline, this feature would be even more valuable. Given the relatively low cost of contributing staff and operating a call center, the investment would provide a high payoff for practitioners, the military, and locals. Participation in such a call center could be an incentive for greater information sharing between organizations that need higher degrees of integration.

A directory feature would enable those without a computer, but with access to a cell phone, to tap into an online database of contacts.[46] This database could also provide information, such as which organizations were lead agencies for water, transport, security, and other sectoral issues in different regions of the country. Further, an up-to-date directory would prove invaluable for practitioners.

A security and tips hotline would provide internationals and locals with a way of retrieving and inputting security information. The tips hotline, which allows anyone to call in security alerts or to share intelligence on threats, proved to be an effective means of gathering information from locals in Iraq.[47] Of course, the validity of this information would be open to question, but in many instances, security information is successfully distributed before it is verified, and proves helpful.[48]

DISTRIBUTE HAND-HELD, DURABLE, AND COST-EFFICIENT COMMUNICATION TOOLS TO LOCAL ORGANIZATIONS OR PEACEKEEPING FORCES. International investment in communications tools and infrastructure would enhance communication. Disseminating (or renting) low-cost communications tools would strengthen information and social networks among locals and expatriates.

Promoting connectivity has a benefit well beyond the immediate financial investment. In austere environments where communications infrastructure is minimal, connecting the maximum number of individuals with simple technology would provide more payoff than waiting for an ideal communications setup. Making sure locals have a means of communication is an essential step in including them in every stage of the reconstruction effort. For example, in Bangladesh, the Grameen phone program gave entire villages phone access by offering low-cost loans for the purchase of cell phones by women, who could then sell call time to villagers for use of the phone.[49]

South Sudan would be an ideal case study because of a growing international presence, a returning population, and a severely limited communications infrastructure.

---

46. These databases are often maintained by OCHA.

47. Donna Miles, "Hotline Succeeding in Foiling Iraqi Insurgents," *American Forces Press Service*, December 28, 2004.

48. ANSO shares security updates before they are verified. It is the primary source of security information for NGOs.

49. For more information on the Village Phone Program, see http://www.grameenphone.com/modules.php?name=Content&pa=showpage&pid=3:11:1.

Alternately, equipping a peacekeeping force like the African Union could improve their effectiveness.[50]

A strategic mix of communication tools should be distributed to increase the capability of the network. This mix would include many radios and cell phones and a few computers and PDAs awarded to the organizations and individuals best suited to strengthen the whole network as central connector points between individuals.[51] This mix could also result in improved synergies. The PDAs could be used to transmit and receive information managed on the computers, phones could be used to call those managing the computer databases and thereby access similar information, and "podcast" type broadcasts and alerts could be sent to the distributed radios.[52]

The Information Communications Technology for Development (ICT4D) field, which helps disconnected communities "leapfrog" into the twenty-first century through improvements in communications infrastructure, could be the appropriate resource for determining appropriate tools. Its many ongoing efforts include the distribution of $100 laptops, wireless technologies, and hand-crank radios, all at low-cost. Consulting with experts in this area would give greater insight into obstacles and opportunities.

Build on Successful Web Sites

A number of excellent networks and Web sites for actors in conflict-prone settings enjoy widespread use; however, some of these efforts reinforce existing stovepipes by targeting only one or two specific communities. These communities should be expanded through user-driven technologies, demonstrating the utility and applicability of open fora. Web sites featuring blogs, wikis, and annotated photo-sharing capacities, using common open-source technologies require minimal management and would provide the most opportunities for dialogue and information sharing.

ADD ADDITIONAL FEATURES. A number of Web sites have the potential to become an important outreach tool to link up individuals and communities of practice, providing user-driven resources to actors across these communities. CSIS recommends adding new capabilities to the following sites:

- Online social networking: DevelopmentEx should incorporate a social networking component to allow registered consultants to search for one another and form communities of practice. Users of MySpace or LinkedIn should identify themselves

---

50. David C. Gompert et al., "Learning from Darfur: Building a Net-Capable African Force to Stop Mass Killing," Center for Technology and National Security Policy, National Defense University, July 2005, http://www.ndu.edu/ctnsp/Def_Tech/DTP%2015%20Darfur.pdf.

51. Global Relief Technologies has developed a hand-held PDA that links to a Virtual Network Operations Center (VNOC). The military and relief workers have relied on this system. This model can become more effective if VNOCs open up their coding and allow multiple users, including those who do not have a subscription to the service, to input data. Databases must be structured so that anyone with access can retrieve information—and retrieve it from trusted sources. For instance, if the military has maps that it wants to share on ReliefWeb using a PDA service, ReliefWeb must have a way to accept this data.

52. After the distribution of these tools, a potential next step for the community would be to establish a central call center for the region.

as a practitioner, scholar, journalist, or uniformed personnel involved in conflict-prone settings.

- Regional- or country-specific Web sites: Sites such as Afghanistan Information Management Service and Sudan Information Gateway should incorporate tools for map-sharing and photo annotation. UN Mission sites should allow for users to upload images.

- User-driven rating systems: DevelopmentGateway, ReliefWeb, and BeyondIntractability should allow users to vote on Top 10 Lists for the best articles, Web sites, blogs, directories, and publications.

- Tagging: Web sites should incorporate ways for users to add keywords and descriptions to sites. Two options would be to feature a "tag this" button to generate awareness of del.icio.us or to follow the UN Development Group's lead and add a keywords option.[53]

- Customization: All Web sites with regularly updated content should incorporate RSS feeds and email alerts to notify users when content of interest is published.[54]

- Chat: Community of practice sites, such as privateforces.com, INPROL, and aidworker.net, should add the capacity for real-time chat between users as in "GmailChat."[55]

- User-contributed content: Policy and academic institutions, country-specific sites, such as those run by UNDP, and news outlets should include wikis and allow users to add information including lists of curricula, training courses, and education seminars.

Many of these features work best with some administration and staffing. Supervision should combine community moderation—where bad content is eliminated and good content is highly rated—as well as formal moderators. Formal moderators guide people to relevant information and assist content producers in adding material to a site.

PUBLICIZE WEB SITES.   Features are only one element of success. Community access is also important. Cross-fertilizing popular sites would increase awareness and build trust between communities. In many cases, the tools practitioners want are available but knowledge of what is already in use is lacking. CSIS recommends the following:

- Convene a "mash-up" conference with 20 technically oriented individuals and 20 practitioners to brainstorm ideas for different sites and catalyze processes of developing and tailoring them for practitioners' specific needs.

- Explore corporate sponsorship of some sites. Consider partnerships to develop "GooglePeace" or "YahooPeace" as a way to increase visibility.

---

53. See http://www.undg.org to see the keyword feature.
54. RSS, Really Simple Syndication, lets users customize Web sites by choosing content sources.
55. For a review of Web sites, see appendix 2.

Conduct Extensive Outreach

Extensive and robust outreach is necessary for the principles and strategic guidelines to make a lasting impact. Ideas that contradict organizational policies and demand changes need advocates to "sell" them. The following outreach strategy would initiate implementation of these recommendations.

BRIEFINGS. CSIS recommends briefing a broad audience to maximize the impact of outreach efforts. Briefings would be held for a select group of influential, high-level officials as well as for larger audiences. A number of organizations should be targeted, including the UN, EU, NATO, OECD, World Bank, international NGOs, and NGO consortia. In addition, government officials from major bilateral donors and governments involved in post-conflict reconstruction should be included.

SPONSOR "INFECTIOUS" MARKETING. The strategic guidelines can be implemented most effectively with "chain-reaction" outreach mechanisms. Outreach should build on and further develop preexisting connections within and between communities. This includes training or academic institutions' alumni lists of practitioners, and rosters of experts.

The most prominent post-conflict reconstruction bloggers should link up to the most popular Web sites. Links directing users to available resources have the potential to drive Internet traffic. In this way, news can rapidly spread across the post-conflict reconstruction blog network. The weekly PCR Brief, available at *www.pcrproject.com,* as well as PCR Project contacts would be used in the first instance to publicize the principles and strategic guidelines to a targeted audience of subscribers.

PUBLICIZE AND PROMOTE COMMUNITIES OF PRACTICE (CoPs). Existing CoPs should expand to include all potential contributors, and new CoPs should be developed in areas where collaboration is weak. Each CoP should be open to inquiries from professionals from other fields who are seeking advice outside their areas of expertise.

Promoting existing CoPs would strengthen ties within and between communities, allowing expertise to develop and deepen. A directory of CoPs would enable segments of different communities to learn about each other's practices and approaches.

Conclusion

These ideas are already becoming a reality. CSIS and its partners have taken important steps to initiate change. PCR Project staff have met with and briefed more than 120 organizations in Washington, D.C., New York, Boston, Germany, the United Kingdom, and Sudan. These meetings have resulted in calls to synchronize connectivity efforts—from linking up isolated communities of practice to networking the numerous projects—with the aim of developing a "one-stop-shop" for stability operations practitioners. Although some organizations have already begun to incorporate the principles and strategic guidelines, much more needs to be done. In particular, how can these ideas actually help people on the ground and lead to better outcomes?

Returning to the Marine discussed in Chapter 1, the benefits of enhanced connectivity become clear. If some of the recommendations in this report were implemented, the Marine would have the technological and professional capacity to access an expanded network, giving him the capacity to "reachback" to development experts anywhere in the world. He would be part of a robust professional community of Civil Affairs Officers, both within the U.S. Marine Corps and other armed forces, that could share advice, opinions, and experiences to help inform his decision in a timely manner. From the field, he would evaluate possible courses of action by way of emails, phone calls, and online discussions.

The Marine's professional community would link into other development communities of practice—such as agricultural development or microfinance—to sound out the best way to spend the CERP funds. He could use photo notes directory populated by his predecessors to identify and familiarize himself with key community leaders and could add his own images and information tags. Prior to entering the field, he could link up, via an online social network, with old colleagues and friends in Iraq or elsewhere, who could provide advice and support. He could seek out experts to evaluate his photos from the project site and help him decide on the most appropriate course of action, particularly when the project's scope lay beyond his expertise. When he returned from the field, he could be a source of advice and information to others.

This scenario is more than an ideal. The military has already recognized the value of increased connectivity and has taken the first steps toward implementation, largely based on concepts of network-centric warfare. For instance, in 2003 an army convoy in southern Iraq came across dead sheep beside the road and feared a chemical attack.[56] Using an in-vehicle computer, the convoy leader accessed an intelligence officer via a chat room who recognized the usual Iraqi practice of dragging dead sheep to the side of the road. The intelligence officer immediately advised that it was not a chemical attack.

The time and expense saved by this connectivity could not have been imagined even during the 1991 Gulf War. Currently, tools with comparable value exist but have not yet been applied. Applications for ongoing operations, as well as for future interventions should be considered. To do so, concurrent efforts are needed, rather than one lead actor taking charge of improving connectivity for everyone. Participatory structures provide the greatest opportunity to capitalize on the ingenuity of multiple practitioners. The first steps already taken are only the beginning of what should be a far-reaching process of transformation across the military, development, humanitarian, and security communities.

This report focuses on improving the effectiveness of international interventions in conflict-prone settings. The findings, however, are applicable to countless other situations, as the problems faced by the international community in conflict-prone settings are not unique. In domestic crisis response many of the same obstacles are encountered: from competing cultures to lack of infrastructure, as was apparent after Hurricane Katrina. Local firemen and National Guardsmen from all over the country may be as different as UN employees and NATO forces. National, state, and local communications systems are no more interoperable than those of international organizations, NGOs, and host governments. Actors in austere environments face the same challenges: natural disasters destroy infrastructure and paralyze communications systems in the same way conflict does.

---

56. Joshua Davis, "If We Run out of Batteries, This War Is Screwed," *Wired*, June 2003, http://wired.com/wired/archive/11.06/battlefield_pr.html.

The principles and strategic guidelines also apply to intelligence gathering, traditional and nontraditional warfare, and even diplomatic relations. The underlying frustrations of bureaucracies and the challenges of international interventions will not change. As communication between groups proliferates, and practitioners access more relevant information through robust networks, all actors can make more informed decisions that will ultimately lead to better outcomes.

Key Web Sites

CROSS-CUTTING

ReliefWeb
www.reliefweb.int

ReliefWeb is the most used Web site for conflict-prone settings, focusing on humanitarian emergencies and disasters. Launched in 1996 and administered by the UN Office for the Coordination of Humanitarian Affairs (OCHA), it averages more than 1 million hits per day, surging to 3 million in the wake of large-scale disasters. ReliefWeb's affiliation with UN OCHA affords it a sense of neutrality as well as a steady stream of donor funding to keep it operational. Its size and exposure are perhaps its best assets. ReliefWeb has no focus on connectivity or cooperation within the response community, and bases its information on UN-approved sources and other standardized news, with no outlet for individual input.

Development Gateway
www.development-gateway.com

Development Gateway was started with support from the World Bank in 2001 and has grown rapidly. It includes some aspects of communities of practice (organized by topic with member login), social network elements, and country gateways (owned and run by individual countries). It has recently started a member directory.

REGIONAL

Afghanistan Information Management System
www.aims.org.af

AIMS is expanding the Afghan government's information management capacity. It also provides this excellent site, a central source of information for both locals and internationals from government, humanitarian, and development organizations. Features include reports, job listings, staff directories, a calendar of events, training courses, and training materials.

Sudan Information Gateway
www.unsudanig.org/

Run by OCHA, this is the most comprehensive online resource on current events in Sudan. Acting as a focal information point for all organizations working in Sudan, it has a contact database, meeting calendar, publications, sector information, and basic facts about Sudan.

SOCIAL

Aidpeople www.aidpeople.org	Rather than producing written resources, Aidpeople is a recently launched online network aiming to connect people. Using features found in successful mainstream online social networks, it helps practitioners track down old friends and colleagues, find new jobs, advertise positions, and seek advice.
Aid Workers Network www.aidworkers.net	This site provides mutual support for practitioners by connecting more than 5,000 individual members who work in PCR. It hopes to become a "one-stop shop" for field workers seeking advice and from those with experience.

PROFESSIONAL

Development Executive Group www.developmentex.com	This is a leading site for development recruiting and tenders, facilitating interchange between donor agencies and development contractors. The Development Executive Group is a for-profit company. It provides research and analysis on funding trends, condenses and compiles procurement and tender notices on a weekly basis, and maintains a large consultant database with CV postings and a job-search function. The Development Executive Group offers neither topical nor regional background information as part of its scope. Full membership for larger organizations is substantial, while smaller businesses can join for lower prices, and individuals can register for free.

COMMUNITIES OF PRACTICE

International Network to Promote the Rule of Law www.inprol.org	A members-only internet-based knowledge network to be launched in mid-2006, the International Network to Promote the Rule of Law is backed by the United States Institute of Peace. It will facilitate the exchange of information between law professionals, allowing "lessons learned" to be turned into "lessons applied."
Company Command www.companycommand.army.mil/ Platoon Leader www.platoonleader.army.mil	These are communities open only to members of the U.S. Army. Company Command started as a way for commanders to quickly provide tips and advice directly to each other, without being delayed by sending messages through the military hierarchy. The sites have since been taken over by the army administration and now feature "online conversations" about how to build more effective army units and become better leaders.
Partnership for Peace Information Management System www.pimswiki.org	The Partnership for Peace (PfP) was launched by NATO in 1994 to establish strong links between NATO and partners in the former Soviet bloc. The PfP has recently established a wiki to make use of "many-to-many" communication (all users can add content, discuss, and answer questions). It hopes to encourage informal, unstructured collaboration and form communities of practice around topics of interests.

RESOURCES (DATA)	
Famine Early Warning System Network www.fews.net	Targeted toward responders to global famine in the humanitarian field, this site provides detailed technical information, including maps and remote sensing outputs, rainfall predictors, monthly reports, and alerts.

RESOURCES (ANALYSIS)	
Beyond Intractability www.beyondintractability.org	Established by the University of Colorado, this site is an open-knowledge database on intractable conflicts. It is targeted toward academic and NGO practitioners and contains more than 4,000 citations to web and print publications, interviews, articles, and news.
Eldis www.eldis.org	A knowledge service provided by the Institute of Development Studies in Sussex (UK), this site is targeted toward NGOs and the private sector. It acts as a portal, linking users to almost 4,500 development organizations, as well as to thousands of reports, job vacancies, news briefs, and training information. It also includes a wiki.
Global Development Network www.gdnet.org	This site, with the goal of improving development research, is aimed at scholars and academics. It provides a comprehensive online library of research generated in developing countries.

TRAINING/COORDINATION	
Learning from International NGOs (LINGOs) www.lingo.org	LINGOs is a consortium of eight major NGOs (including Care, CRS, World Vision, Mercy Corps, and Save the Children) focusing on poverty alleviation and emergency response. LINGOs engages partner organizations—companies and associations working in the field of technology-assisted learning—to provide expert help, and creates economies of scale by coordinating member needs and sharing training outcomes.

Web Site Review

Web site	Function
CROSS-CUTTING	
Development Gateway www.developmentgateway.com	**RESOURCE/PORTAL:** DG provides a space for communities to share experiences on development efforts. Four main goals: (1) increase knowledge sharing; (2) Enhance development effectiveness; (3) Improve public sector transparency; (4) Build local capacity and empower communities.
ReliefWeb www.reliefweb.int	**RESOURCE/PORTAL:** UN site that aims to serve as source of information for different actors in humanitarian situations, particularly regarding status of operations, other actors, and funding.
REGIONAL	
Afghanistan Information Management Service (AIMS) www.aims.org.af	**PORTAL/RESOURCE:** Provides information services to the government, humanitarian, and development community in Afghanistan. This is Afghanistan's version of the HIC (Humanitarian Information Center) Web site (*see below*).
Anti-Trafficking in Persons in Asia (TipInAsia) Portal www.tipinasia.info	**RESOURCE/PORTAL:** Country specific information regarding human trafficking (for Thailand, East Timor, Cambodia), as well as informational resources and anti-trafficking news.
Asia-Pacific Area Network (APAN) www.apan-info.net	**PORTAL/RESOURCE:** Site offering information resources and a collaborative planning environment as a means to greater defense interaction, confidence building and enhanced security cooperation in the Asia-Pacific region
Operational Activities and Security Information System (OASIS) Iraq *(in development)* **Vietnam Veterans of America Foundation** www.vvaf.org	**RESOURCE/PORTAL:** Intended to share security information with civilian and military actors to allow for safer program application.

Relief Information System for Earthquakes—Pakistan (RISEPAK)
www.risepak.com/Default.aspx

PORTAL: For the Pakistan earthquake. Coordinates logistical relief efforts on a flexible and searchable platform: receives, collates, and posts information on access, damage and relief on a village level.

South Asia Terrorism Portal
www.satp.org

RESOURCE: Listing of documents, background information, terrorist-groups and news related to terrorism in South Asia.

Sri Lanka Tsunami Relief Portal
infoshareaid.blogspot.com
and www.infoshare.org/
doc_view.php?record_id=34

PORTAL: Lists sites that are relevant to tsunami relief and organizes them according to their focus, as a way to link responders and create a more unified approach.

Sudan Information Gateway
www.unsudanig.org/

PORTAL: A focal point for all organizations working in Sudan.

Wikipedia - Iraq
en.wikipedia.org/wiki/Iraq

RESOURCE/ENCYCLOPEDIA/WIKI: User-contributed information on Iraq.

SOCIAL

Aidpeople
www.aidpeople.org

ONLINE NETWORK: Assisting people who work in the aid and development community to connect, including with former friends and colleagues.

Aid Workers Network
www.aidworkers.net

RESOURCE/PORTAL: Proclaimed "one-stop-shop" for field workers needing advice or resources to help with their work. The Web site provides links to other online resources recommended by field workers, as well as publishing original content where none exists. The network is run by aid workers.

PROFESSIONAL

Alliance for Conflict Transformation (ACT)
www.conflicttransformation.org

RESOURCE: Information on jobs, scholarships, grants and events in peace and conflict resolution, international development, humanitarian relief and related fields.

Collaborative Learning Projects & the Collaborative for Development Action, Inc.
www.cdainc.com

RESOURCE: Pool of German civilian professionals qualified to work in peace operations that international organizations can draw from.

Development Executive Group
www.developmentex.com

RESOURCE/COORDINATION/NEWS/JOB LISTINGS: Provides business intelligence reports for development contractors.

Development Experience Clearing House
http://dec.usaid.gov/

RESOURCE: Run by USAID, this site is the largest online resource for USAID-funded technical and program documentation.

Field Coordination and Support System (FCSS), UN OCHA
http://ochaonline.un.org

ORGANIZATION INFORMATION: Information relating to the operation of OCHA's FCSS; main purpose is to develop, prepare and maintain stand-by capacity for rapid deployment to sudden-onset emergencies

COMMUNITIES OF PRACTICE

Company Command
www.companycommand.army.mil
and
Platoon Leader
www.platoonleader.army.mil

RESOURCE/PORTAL: Promotes sharing of lessons-learned with user-driven message boards, background information, and subject forums covering a range of command situations.

Frameweb
www.frameweb.org

RESOURCE/PORTAL: To create a knowledge sharing network of natural resource professionals.

Good Humanitarian Donorship Initiative
www.reliefweb.int/ghd

ORGANIZATION: To address the lack of consensus on how governments can best mobilize humanitarian aid, work in concert and create mechanisms to harmonize government approaches to aid.

Humanitarian Practice Network
www.odihpn.org/index.asp

RESOURCE: An independent forum where field workers, managers and policymakers in the humanitarian sector share information, analysis. It aims to improve the performance of humanitarian action by contributing to individual and institutional learning.

Microlinks
www.microlinks.org

RESOURCE/PORTAL: A knowledge sharing Web site designed to improve the impact of USAID microenterprise projects, including microfinance, remittances and microinsurance.

Partnership for Peace Information Management System (PIMSWiki)
www.pims.org

RESOURCE/WIKI/COORDINATION: Allows colleagues who work in the *PfP/NATO* community to share their knowledge for security cooperation and interoperability. Upcoming exercises, meeting agendas, background information databases, discussions, best practices, lessons learned, and local knowledge can be shared and added by users.

RESOURCES (DATA)

Famine Early Warning System Network (FEWS)
www.fews.net

RESOURCE: Detailed technical data for organizations responding to famines.

Geographic Information Support Team (GIST)
https://gist.itos.uga.edu

RESOURCE (MAPS): Inter-agency initiative that promotes the use of geographic data standards and geographical information systems (GIS) in support of humanitarian relief operations.

Respond
www.respond-int.org/Respond/

RESOURCE: Maps, satellite imagery and geographic information

RESOURCES (ANALYSIS)

Beyond Intractability
www.beyondintractability.org

RESOURCE: (related to CRIS *below*) A general knowledge base, particularly dealing with ethnic/civil/societal/racial skirmishes.

Center of Excellence in Disaster Management and Humanitarian Assistance (COEDMHA)
www.coe-dmha.org

RESOURCE: The COEDMHA provides continuously updated materials and resources to promote effective civil-military management in international humanitarian assistance, disaster response and peacekeeping. Funded by USG.

Conflict Resolution Information Source (CRIS)
www.crinfo.org

RESOURCE: Approximately 25 000 conflict resolution resources (not specific to international conflict).

Eldis Gateway to Development Information
www.eldis.org

PORTAL/RESOURCE: A knowledge service provided by the Institute of Development Studies, Sussex.

FIRST Fact-finding Database
first.sipri.org/index.php

DATABASE/RESOURCE: A searchable database of relevant facts for individual countries.

Global Development Network (GDN)
www.gdnet.org

RESOURCE: Provides the electronic link to GDN's work in improving development research worldwide.

Global Policy Forum
www.globalpolicy.org

RESOURCE: Source of documents related to the monitoring of policy making at the United Nations, accountability of global decisions, and issues of international peace and justice.

Global Security
http://www.globalsecurity.org/

RESOURCE: GS provides information, news, and analysis on topics ranging from the U.S. military, WMDs and intelligence to homeland security, specifically in relation to the reduction of reliance on WMDs.

Human Security Gateway
www.humansecuritygateway.info

RESOURCE/NEWS: HSG provides news, resources (articles, reports), links to other portals; all sorted regionally and topically.

International AIDS Economics Network
www.iaen.org

RESOURCE/FORUM: Compilation of resources, event listings, conferences and forums for AIDS-related analyses of economics.

International Crisis Group
www.icg.org

RESOURCE/DATABASE. The International Crisis Group is an independent, non-profit, non-governmental organization, with over 110 staff members on five continents, working through field-based analysis and high-level advocacy to prevent and resolve deadly conflict.

International Relations and Security Network (The Center for Security Studies, Switzerland)
www.isn.ethz.ch/index.cfm

RESOURCE: Collection of specialized information for the international relations and security community.

Joint Doctrine Branch
www.dtic.mil/doctrine

RESOURCE: Promotes joint doctrine awareness and manages the development of joint doctrine for improved joint, interagency, and multinational interoperability and to enhance CINC war fighting capabilities.

KM World www.kmworld.com	**KNOWLEDGE MANAGEMENT:** Content, document and knowledge management information.
Open Source Information System (OSIS) http://www.fas.org/irp/program/disseminate/osis.htm	**RESOURCE:** Access to open-source information for military and intelligence personnel.
Peace Keeping and Stability Operations Institute (PKSOI) www.carlisle.army.mil/usacsl/divisions/pksoi/default.htm	**RESOURCE/TRAINING:** Provides materials related to military and civil-military aspects of peace keeping and stability operations. Designed to meet the future needs of the U.S. Army and the U.S. military primarily.
Storming Media www.stormingmedia.us	**RESOURCE:** a private, independent reseller of unclassified Pentagon and other U.S. federal government reports on a wide range of subjects.
UN Humanitarian Information Centers (HICs) www.humanitarianinfo.org	**RESOURCE/PORTAL:** Supports the coordination of humanitarian assistance through the provision of information products and services. HICs support the decision-making process at headquarters and field level by contributing to the creation of a common framework for information management within the humanitarian community.
Women, Peace and Security Portal www.womenwarpeace.org	**RESOURCE:** A Web site run by UNIFEM (United National Development Fund for Women) dedicated to issues of gender in war, peace and security.
World Bank Institute, Knowledge Sharing www.worldbank.org/ks	**KNOWLEDGE MANAGEMENT:** Presents the World Bank's approach to knowledge management and information sharing, both within the WB and through outreach to donors.
World Bank Rapid Response Unit, Conflict Affected Countries rru.worldbank.org/Themes/ConflictAffectedCountries	**RESOURCE:** Central resource for World Bank information on operating in conflict affected countries including research, education, discussion, and news, with a focus on private sector development in these areas.

TRAINING

Active Learning Network for Accountability and Performance in Humanitarian Action (ALNAP) www.alnap.org	**RESOURCE:** To improve performance across the humanitarian sector by upgrading and standardizing evaluative practices.
Care Academy www.careacademy.org	**TRAINING/KNOWLEDGE MANAGEMENT:** Care Academy's mission is to identify and develop staff learning opportunities that: educate and train staff on mission-critical skills; enhance leadership capabilities of individuals within organizations; and communicate clear standards for CARE staff through CARE-specific orientations and knowledge sharing.

Global Development Learning Network (GDLN) wwww.gdln.org	**ORGANIZATION INFORMATION:** A global partnership of learning centers supported by the World Bank using advanced technology to connect people working in development.
Learning for International NGOs (LINGO) www.lingo.org	**TRAINING/COORDINATION/ KNOWLEDGE MANAGEMENT:** LINGOs is a consortium of learning professionals from eight major NGOs (including Care, CRS, World Vision, Mercy Corps, and Save the Children) who collaborate, share and learn. LINGOs also engages partner organizations - companies and associations working in the field of technology assisted learning - to provide expert help and other support aimed at alleviating poverty and effectively responding to emergencies.
People in Aid www.peopleinaid.org	**RESOURCE:** To enhance the impact of aid by improving human resource management.

COORDINATION

Aid Harmonization & Alignment www.aidharmonization.org	**RESOURCE/COORDINATION:** To increase aid harmonization, by both donors and implementers. Gives a general overview of countries and donor organizations, who is doing what where, and information on recent donor coordination events
Coordination SUD (Solidarite, Urgence, Developpement) www.coordinationsud.org	**RESOURCE/PORTAL:** A French umbrella organization that operates web portal for French NGOs
CPR Network http://cpr.web.cern.ch/cpr/	**RESOURCE/PORTAL:** Donor collaboration on conflict prevention and post conflict reconstruction, tools, events and library.
Global Disaster Alert and Response Coordination System (GDAS)—UN OCHA http://www.gdacs.org/	**PORTAL/ALERT SYSTEM:** Web-based platform for alerts about major sudden-onset disasters and to facilitate the coordination of international relief response.
Groupe Urgence, Rehabilitation, Developpement (URD) www.urd.org	**RESOURCE:** Aims to bridge gaps in the French NGO community.
Humanitarian Accountability Partnership-International (HAP-I) www.hapinternational.org	**RESOURCE:** To ensure that all agencies doing humanitarian work reach intended recipients and are accountable to them.
Humaninet www.humaninet.org	**TECHNOLOGY RESOURCE:** Looks for and distributes best practices, and field results in global information and communication technologies (ICT). Also seeks to provide NGOs with equipment and updates to enhance ICT in the field.
InterAction www.interaction.org	**ORGANIZATION/RESOURCE:** Works to coordinate efforts of U.S.-based NGOs that work internationally so as to maximize impact of policy and on the ground.

Net Hope
www.nethope.org

ORGANIZATION INFORMATION: For ICT collaboration with NGOs. Global initiative of several collaborating international NGOs to increase coordination in ICT for disaster relief, humanitarian emergencies etc.

NGO Connect.NET
www.ngoconnect.net

RESOURCE/PORTAL: NGO Connect.NET is funded by USAID's Capable Partners Program. The Web site acts as an information bank of NGO practices and aims to link NGO community.

OECD Development Assistance Committee (OECD-DAC)
www.oecd.org/dac

ORGANIZATION: Created to coordinate donor assistance to developing world.

Sphere Project, The: Disaster Relief
www.sphereproject.org

RESOURCE: A handbook for improving collaboration, quality and accountability in disaster relief.

UN Disaster Assessment and Coordination (UN DAC)
http://ochaonline.un.org/webpage.asp?MenuID=2893&Page=552

ORGANIZATION INFORMATION: On request of a disaster-stricken country, the UNDAC team can be deployed within hours to carry out rapid assessment of priority needs and to support national authorities and the United Nations Resident Coordinator to coordinate international relief.

UN Inter-Agency Standing Committee (IASC)
www.humanitarianinfo.org/iasc

ORGANIZATION: To provide a forum that brings together a range of UN and non-UN humanitarian partners to coordinate response.

United Nations Joint Logistics Center
www.unjlc.org

RESOURCE: Center for information relating to UN missions (travel, fuel, infrastructure etc.) run by the UN's World Food Program.

UN Special Committee on Peacekeeping Operations (C-34)
www.un.org/Depts/dpko/ctte/CTTEE.htm

ORGANIZATION: To develop coordinated approaches to issues of peacekeeping.

Information Needs

Interviews, surveys, and focus groups in the United States and abroad with more than 120 practitioners, uniformed personnel, government employees, civil society organizations, diplomats, consultants, and academics revealed a diverse range of responses to the question "What is your greatest information need in the field?"

NEED	DESCRIPTION
Handover notes	High staff turnover means that institutional memory is poor and critical knowledge is often lost.
Security briefings and up-to-date security information	In particular NGOs feel left out when there is an overarching security organization (such as the U.S. military or the UN) that does not share its security information.
Timely analysis	Practitioners are bombarded with updates of project activities but there are few sources that provide reliable interpretation of data.
Directories	High staff turnover renders contact lists quickly obsolete. High-level staff can be easier to find, but less accessible, whereas junior- to mid-level staff are harder to track down. Horizontal connections between counterparts in different organizations are difficult to make.
Data on local population needs	First responders need detailed information on the needs of the local population, such as health characteristics, local aid capacities, and the local agencies' available resources.
Program design and funding procedures	Local actors emphasize their lack of knowledge about who designs programs and controls funding. Many local NGOs feel excluded from strategic decisions made at the country, and even sub-national, level.
Centralized database for country assessments	A diverse range of actors conduct numerous assessments on a wide range of topics, but accessing the final reports is often difficult, as they are not collected in one place.
Calendars of events geared toward specific issues	Keeping track of even one area of expertise can be difficult with many disparate actors working in one subject area.

Maps	Host government maps are often outdated and may not reflect losses to infrastructure due to conflict.
Lists of local and regional organizations	Often even the government does not know how many, or what type of, organizations are working in a given area, nor the programs they are implementing.
Notification of new decisions by local authorities	Workers in the field are often not kept informed in a timely fashion of changes in the regulatory environment.

Board of Advisers

Col. John Agoglia
U.S. Army Peacekeeping and Stability Operations Institute

Laura Bailey
The World Bank Group

Paul Bartel
Humanitarian Information Unit
U.S. State Department

Dave Buckley
The Triple-I Corporation

Claudio Cioffi-Revilla
George Mason University

Kami Dar
Development Executive Group

Alan Davis
Humanitarian Information Unit
U.S. State Department

Beth deGrasse
United States Institute of Peace

Ron Dysvick
The Triple-I Corporation

Greg Elin
Footnotes

Adam Fisk
Last Bamboo

Bailey Hand
Office of the Secretary of Defense (Policy)
Department of Defense

Bernard Harborne
The World Bank Group

Chip Hauss
Search for Common Ground

Kevin Heald
Ennovex

J.C. Herz

David Heyman
Center for Strategic and International Studies

Victoria Holt
The Stimson Center

Robert Jenkins
Office of Transition Initiatives
U.S. Agency for International Development

Robert Jimenez
Global Strategies Group

Dennis King
Humanitarian Information Unit
U.S. State Department

Spanky Kirsch
U.S. Department of Defense

Frank Kramer
National Defense University

Stephen Lennon
International Organization for Migration

Julia Loughran
ThoughtLink, Inc

Curt Mattingly
CherryRoad Technologies

Kara McDonald
*Office of the Coordinator for Reconstruction
and Stabilization
U.S. Department of State*

Michael McNerney
U.S. Department of Defense

Johanna Mendelson Forman
United Nations Foundation

Earnest Paylor
U.S. Department of Defense

Mike Pereira
Development Gateway

Douglas Price
Last Bamboo

Charles Santangelo
CherryRoad Technologies

Sarah Schmidt
Development Alternatives, Inc.

Tammy Schulz
*Peacekeeping and Stability Operations
Institute*

Mike Sherman
*Science Applications International
Corporation*

Mike Sponder

J. Alexander Thier
United States Institute of Peace

Duncan Watts
Columbia University

Wade Weems
Williams & Connolly LLP

Michael Wenger

Jennifer Widner
Princeton University

David Yang
UN Development Program

Organizations Consulted

International Organizations

Headquarters

International Organization for Migration (IOM)

United Nations Children's Fund (UNICEF)

United Nations Department of Peacekeeping Operations (DPKO), Best Practices Unit

United Nations Development Group Office (UNDGO)

United Nations Development Program (UNDP)

 Bureau for Crisis Prevention and Recovery

 Office of Legal and Procurement Support

UN Office for Project Services (UNOPS)

United Nations Office of the Coordinator of Humanitarian Affairs (OCHA)

The World Bank Group

Sudan

African Union Mission in Sudan (AMIS)

International Organization for Migration (IOM)

United Nations Mission in Sudan (UNMIS)

United Nations Office of the Coordinator of Humanitarian Affairs (OCHA)

 Information Management Unit

 Project Monitoring and Evaluation Unit

United Nations Development Program UNDP

United Nations Field Security Coordination Office

Nongovernmental Organizations (NGOs)

Americares

CARE

Catholic Relief Services

CHF International

Dawa Islamiya

Food for the Hungry

Grand Africa Media Service Company

HELP e.V. (Bosnia)

Institute for International Education

Interaction

International Committee of the Red Cross

International Orthodox Christian Charities

International Rescue Committee

Islamic Relief Worldwide

Khartoum Monitor

Medair

Médecins Sans Frontières (MSF)

Mennonite Central Committee (Bosnia-Herzegovina)

Mercy Corps International

National Endowment for Democracy

Oxfam

Relief International
Save the Children
Search for Common Ground
Sudan Inter-Religious Council
Sudan Self-Help Foundation

SUDIA
Transparency International (Bosnia)
War Child
Welthungerhilfe

Research Organizations/Academic Institutions

Cebrowski Institute
Center for Strategic and International Studies
Chatham House
Columbia University
Eastern Mennonite University
George Mason University
George Washington University
Harvard Berkman Center for Internet & Society

Henry L. Stimson Center
Massachusetts Institute of Technology
Partnership for Effective Peacekeeping
Princeton University
Royal United Services Institute for Defence and Security Studies (United Kingdom)
U.S. Institute of Peace
United Nations Foundation
University of Maryland

U.S. Government

Agency for International Development
    Bureau of Conflict Management and Mitigation
    Office of Transition Initiatives
Army
    CERDEC
    Civil Affairs
    Corps of Engineers
Center for Army Lessons Learned
Department of Defense
    Office of the Assistant Secretary of Defense (Homeland Defense)
    Office of the Assistant Secretary of Defense (Public Affairs)
    Office of the Deputy Under Secretary of Defense (Industrial Policy)
    Office of the Secretary of Defense, Networks and Information Integration
    Stability Operations Low Intensity Conflict

Department of Homeland Security
Institute for Defense Analyses
Joint Forces Command
Joint Rapid Acquisition Cell
National Defense University
Naval Postgraduate School
Marine Corps
    Security Cooperation Education and Training Center
    Small Wars Center for Excellence
Open Source Information Service
Peace Corps
Peacekeeping and Stability Operations Institute

State Department

E-Government
Humanitarian Information Unit

Office of the Coordinator for Reconstruction
and Stabilization

Contractors

AfEx
BearingPoint
Chemonics International
CherryRoad Technologies
Computer Sciences Corporation
Development Alternatives, Inc
Development Executive Group
DFI Government Services
Global Relief Technologies

GP Worldwide
International Resources Group
Kjer and Kjer
RAI
RTI International
Thoughtlink, Inc.
Triple-I Corporation
Unity Resources Group
USAID Consultant

Other

Blueforce LLC
Business Executives for National Security
UK Department for International
Development (DFID)
Evidence Based Research, Inc.
Global Strategies Group LLC
Google
Horizontal Fusion

Last Bamboo
Management Systems International
MorganFranklin Corporation
My Virtual Model
Ramsey Decision Theoretics
Shinkuro, Inc.
SkinnyCorps

Bibliography

Aschenbrenner, Aaron LT. "International Interagency Collaborative Environment Network." Presentation, U.S. European Command, May 9, 2006.

Bates, James A. *The War on Terrorism: Countering Global Insurgency in the 21ˢᵗ Century.* JSOU Report 05-08. Hurlburt Field: JSOU Press, 2005.

Baum, Dan. "Battle Lessons: What the Generals Don't Know." *New Yorker.* January 17, 2005.

Blackledge, David N. Brigadier General. "Coalition Provisional Authority Briefing." January 14, 2004. http://www.defenselink.mil/transcripts/2004/tr20040114-1144.html.

Brooks, Doug. "Private Military Service Providers: Africa's Welcome Pariahs." Chap. 1, essay 4. In *Nouveaux Mondes*, no. 10, edited by Laurent Bachelor, 69–86. Geneva: Centre de Recherches Entreprises et Societes, 2002. http://www.ipoaonline.org/uploads/brooks-africas%20welcome%20pariahs.pdf.

Coalition Warrior Interoperability Demonstration. *Joint Warrior Interoperability Demonstration 2004 Final Report UST 01.13: Secure Wide Area Response Management, 2004.* http://www.cwid.js.mil/public/cwid05fr/htmlfiles/u113intr.html.

Call, Charles. "Institutionalizing Peace: A Review of Post-Conflict Peacebuilding Concepts and Issues for DPA." United Nations Department of Political Affairs, January 31, 2005.

Carnahan, Michael, William Durch, and Scott Gilmore. *Economic Impact of Peacekeeping: Final Report.* Peace Dividend Trust, March 20, 2006. http://pbpu.unlb.org/pbpu/library/EIP_FINAL_Report_March20_2006doc.pdf

Dysvick, Ronald. "BCKS Next Steps." Triple-I, February 16, 2006.

Felter et al. *Harmony and Disharmony: Exploiting al-Qua'ida's Organizational Vulnerability.* Combating Terrorism Center, Department of Social Sciences, U.S. Military Academy, February 14, 2006. http://iis-db.stanford.edu/pubs/21057/Harmony_and_Disharmony-CTC.pdf

Flournoy, Michèle, and Shawn Brimley. "Strategic Planning for National Security: A New Project Solarium." *Joint Forces Quarterly* 42 (2006): 80–86.

Deputy Secretary of Defense. Memorandum. "DSB Report: Institutionalizing Stability Operations Within DoD." January 22, 2006.

Deputy Secretary of Defense. Memorandum. "2005 Quadrennial Defense Review Execution Roadmaps." January 5, 2006.

DFI International Government Services. "Civil Affairs and Regional Studies Knowledge Center: Potential Support to USACAPOC." Prepared for Col. Matt Artero and Rebecca Linder. November 9, 2005.

Dobbins, James, et al. "America's Role in Nation-Building: From Germany to Iraq." RAND, 2003.

Dobbins, James, et. al. "The UN's Role in Nation-Building: From the Congo to Iraq." RAND, 2005.

Evans, Philip, and Bob Wolf. "Collaboration Rules." *Harvard Business Review* (July 2005): 96.

Giles, Jim. "Internet Encyclopedias Go Head to Head." *Nature* 438 (December 15, 2005): 900–901.

Gompert, David C., et al. "Learning from Darfur: Building a Net-Capable African Force to Stop Mass Killing." Center for Technology and National Security Policy, National Defense University, July 2005. http://www.ndu.edu/ctnsp/Def_Tech/ DTP%2015% 20Darfur.pdf.

Grissom, Adam, and David Ochmanek. "Prosecuting the Long War: Getting from Strategy to Operations and Requirements." Presentation, April 2006.

Holohan, Anne. *UNDP: The Challenge of Becoming a Network Organization.* Social Science Research Council. http://www.ssrc.org/programs/itic/publications/ civsocandgov/holohanpolicy2.pdf

_____. "Cooperation and Coordination in an International Intervention: The Use of Information and Communication Technologies in Kosovo." *Information Technologies and International Development* 1, no. 1 (fall 2003): 19–39.

_____. *Networks of Democracy: Lessons from Kosovo, for Afghanistan, Iraq, and Beyond.* Stanford, Calif.: Stanford University Press, 2005.

Holshek, Chistopher J. *Civil-Military Measures of Effectiveness: What's It All About?* Prepared for Cornwallis Group X, July 6, 2005.

Humanitarian Information Unit. *HIU Highlights Report No. 11*, October 1, 2005– December 31, 2005. http://www.ndu.edu/ITEA/storage/685/ HIU%20Highlights%2011.pdf.

_____. *HIU Highlights Report No. 12*, January 1, 2006–March 31, 2006. http:// www.ndu.edu/ITEA/storage/695/Highlights%20No%20%2012%20- %20Gen%20Dist.pdf.

Institute for Defense Analyses. *Glossary: Terminology Related to Operations Involving Civilian and Military Resources.* Working Draft, January 26, 2006.

InterAction. "Private Voluntary Organization Standards." Presentation, 2005. http:// www.interaction.org/files.cgi/3098_PVO_powerpoint_2005.ppt.

Jebb, Cindy R., and Madelfia A. Abb. "Human Security and Good Governance: A Living Systems Approach to Understanding and Combating Terrorism." In *The Making of a Terrorist: Recruitment, Training, and Root Causes*, vol. 3, edited by J.F. Forrest. Westport, Conn.: Praeger Security International, 2006.

Kent, Randolph, et al. *The Future of Humanitarian Assistance: The Role of the United Nations.* New York: United Nations, 2004.

King, Dennis. "Information Technology: Best Practices and Recommendations." U.S. Department of State, Humanitarian Information Unit. SMART Technical Meeting Presentation, June 24, 2005. http://www.smartindicators.org/workshop/meeting/ presentations/SMART_King.ppt.

Kirsch, Spanky. "OASD/NII CSMP." Presentation, December 7, 2005.

Kramer, Frank . "In the Eye of the Storm: A Primer on ICT Support for Civil-Military Coordination in Stabilization & Reconstruction and Disaster Relief Operations." National Defense University. Discussion Draft, October 27, 2005. http://www.ndu.edu/CTNSP/S&RWorkshop_Oct05/ICT%20SR%20Primer% 20(discussion%20draft).doc.

Lessons Learned Information Sharing. "Portland, Oregon's Regional Alliances for Infrastructure and Network security (RAINS)-Net: Connect and Protect." April 20, 2005. http://www.swanisland.net/docs/Connect%20and%20Protect%20LLIS% 20Apr05.pdf

Langewiesche, Wiliam. "The Lessons of ValuJet 592." *Atlantic Online*, March 1998.

_____. "Columbia's Last Flight: The Inside Story of the Investigation—and the Catastrophe It Laid Bare." *Atlantic Online*, November 2003. http:// www.theatlantic.com/doc/print/200311/langewiesche.

Levy, Steven, and Brad Stone. "The New Wisdom of the Web." *Newsweek*, April 3, 2006.

Loughran, Julia. "Institutional Issues and Innovative Solutions for Bringing People Together." National Defense University, April 27, 2006.

Malcolm Gladwell. *The Tipping Point: How Little Things Can Make a Big Difference.* Boston, Mass.: Back Bay Books, 2002.

_____. "The Cellular Church: How Rick Warren Built His Ministry." *New Yorker*, September 12, 2005.

McGuire, Mike, and Derek Slater. *Consumer Taste Sharing is Driving the Online Music Business and Democratizing Culture.* The Berkman Center for Internet & Society at Harvard Law School. December 13, 2005. http://cyber.law.harvard.edu/home/ uploads/511/11-ConsumerTasteSharing.pdf.

McMahon, Patrice C. "Ethnic Peace in the East: Transnational Networks and the CSCE/OSCE." *Ethnopolitics* 5, no. 2 (June 2006): 101–123. http://taylorandfrancis.metapress.com/openurl.asp?genre=article&eissn=1744-9065&volume=5&issue=2&spage=101.

McMahon, Patrice C. *Taming Ethnic Hatred: Ethnic Cooperation and Transnational Networks in Eastern Europe.* Syracuse, N.Y.: Syracuse University Press, forthcoming.

Markle Foundation. *Creating a Trusted Network for Homeland Security: Second Report for the Markle Foundation Task Force,* 2003. http://www.markle.org/downloadable_assets/nstf_report2_full_report.pdf.

Miles, Donna. "Hotline Succeeding in Foiling Iraqi Insurgents." American Forces Press Service, December 28, 2004.

Mishra, Shridhar Mubaraq, et al. "Economic Analysis of Networking Technologies for Rural Developing Regions." September, 2005. http://www.cs.berkeley.edu/~lakme/wine.pdf.

OASIS—Operational Activities and Security Information System. "RAINS Regional Alliances for Infrastructure and Network Security Fact Sheet." March 10, 2006. http://www.oregonrains.org/files/PDF/RAINS_Fact_Sheet.pdf.

PBS. "Battle Plan under Fire: The Immutable Nature of War." December 17, 2003. http://www.pbs.org/wgbh/nova/wartech/nature.html.

Pew Internet Global Attitudes Project. "Truly a World Wide Web: Globe Going Digital." *2005 PEW Global Attitudes Survey.* February 21, 2006. http://pewglobal.org/reports/pdf/251.pdf.

Shirky, Clay. "Ontology is Overrated: Categories, Links, and Tages." *Clay Shirky's Writings about the Internet: Economics & Culture, Media & Community.* http://shirky.com/writings/ontology_overrated.html.

Schulenburg, Michael. *OSCE's Management Reforms and IRMA (2002–2005): Final Report.* Organization for Security and Cooperation in Europe, February 2005.

Stavridis, James. "Deconstructing War." Proceedings, December 2005. http://esc.hanscom.af.mil/ESCPA/The%20Integrator/2005/December/12152005/12152005-18.htm.

Surowiecki, James. *The Wisdom of Crowds: Why the Many Are Smarter than the Few and How Collective Wisdom Shapes Business, Economies, Societies and Nations.* New York: Doubleday, 2004.

Thibodeau, Patrick. *Defense Department Looks to Be More "Netcentric": It's Hoping to Learn from How Private Companies Solve Problems.* Computerworld, November 9, 2005. http://www.w2cog.org/documents/051109%20Computerworld.pdf.

Tillson, John C.F., et al. *Learning to Adapt to Asymmetric Threats.* Institute for Defense Analysis, August, 2005. http://www.d-n-i.net/fcs/pdf/learning_to_adapt.pdf.

Defense Acquisition University. "Portals, Collaboration & Content Management Conference Trip Report," November 17, 2005. https://acc.dau.mil/ CommunityBrowser.aspx?id=22266.

Ulwick, Anthony W. "Turn Customer Input into Innovation." *Harvard Business Review* 80, no. 1. (January 2002).

_____. "Defense Science Board 2004 Summer Study: Transition to and from Hostilities." Office of the Under Secretary of Defense for Acquisition, Technology, and Logistics, December 2004. http://www.acq.osd.mil/dsb/reports/2004-12-DSB_SS_Report_Final.pdf.

_____. "Implementing the Stability Operations Directive: OSD Policy SO/LIC Stability Operations." Unclassified Draft, December 14, 2005.

_____. "Directive 3000.05: Military Support for Stability, Security, Transition, and Reconstruction (SSTR) Operations." November 28, 2005. http://www.dtic.mil/ whs/directives/corres/pdf/d300005_112805/d300005p.pdf.

_____. "Report of the Defense Science Board Task Force on Institutionalizing Stability Operations Within DoD." Office of the Under Secretary of Defense for Acquisition, Technology, and Logistics, September 2005. http://stinet.dtic.mil/cgibin/ GetTRDoc?AD=ADA441078&Location=U2&doc=GetTRDoc.pdf.

_____. "Defense Science Board Summer Study on Transformation: A Progress Assessment, Volume I." Office of the Under Secretary of Defense for Acquisition, Technology, and Logistics, February 2006

United Nations. "A More Secure World: Our Shared Responsibility." Report of the Secretary-General's High Level Panel on Threats Challenges and Change, January 20, 2005.

U.S. Department of State. "Communities@State: Theory and Practice of Communities of Practice." Presentation, April 27, 2006.

U.S. Government Accountability Office. "Report to the Subcommittee on Oversight and Investigations, Committee on International Relations, House of Representatives: Peacekeeping: Cost Comparison of Actual UN and Hypothetical U.S. Operations in Haiti." February 2006. http://www.acq.osd.mil/dsb/reports/ 2006-02DSB_SS_Transformation_Report_Vol_1.pdf.

Uvin, Peter. *Aiding Violence: The Development Enterprise in Rwanda.* West Hartford, Conn.: Kumarian Press, 1998.

Van Deventer, Fulco. "The Role of Civil Society in the Prevention of Armed Conflict: Issue Paper on Understanding Networks." Global Partnership for the Prevention of Armed Conflict. October 2004. http://www.gppac.org/documents/GPPAC/ Research/Role_of_CS_in_CP/Issue_paper_on_Networking_Oct_2004.doc.

Verini, James. "Will Success Spoil MySpace.com?" *Vanity Fair.* http://www.vanityfair.com/commentary/content/articles/060308roco01.

Von Hippel, Eric. *Democratizing Innovation*. Cambridge, Mass.: MIT Press, 2005.

Watts, Duncan. "Decentralized Intelligence: What Toyota Can Teach the 9/11 Commission about Intelligence Gathering." *Slate*, August 5, 2004.

Wells, Linton. "The HUB: Technology for Collaborative Information Environments." Office of the Assistant Secretary of Defense, Networks and Information Integration. March 9, 2006.

Wentz, Larry. "Information and Communication Technologies for Civil-Military Coordination in Disaster Relief and Stabilization and Reconstruction." Center for Technology and National Security Policy, National Defense University, July 2006. http://www.ndu.edu/ctnsp/Def_Tech/DTP31%20ICT%20Primer.pdf

Wilson, Clay. "Network Centric Warfare: Background and Oversight Issues for Congress." Congressional Research Service Report for Congress, June 2, 2004.